T0116138

THE FREE PRESS

New York   London   Toronto   Sydney   Singapore

The STATE *of* AMERICANS

THIS GENERATION AND THE NEXT

Urie Bronfenbrenner

Peter McClelland

Elaine Wethington

Phyllis Moen

Stephen J. Ceci

with

Helene Hembrooke, Pamela A. Morris, and Tara L. White

THE FREE PRESS
A Division of Simon & Schuster Inc.
1230 Avenue of the Americas
New York, NY 10020

THE FREE PRESS and colophon are trademarks
of Simon & Schuster Inc.

Manufactured in the United States of America

10 9 8 7 6 5 4 3 2 1

Library of Congress Cataloging-in-Publication Data

The state of Americans : this generation and the next / Urie
    Bronfenbrenner . . . [et al.].
        p.   cm.
    Includes bibliographical references.
    ISBN 978-1-4165-7697-6   ISBN 1-4165-7697-5
    1. United States—Social conditions—1980–   2. United States—
Social policy.   I. Bronfenbrenner, Urie, 1917–
HN59.2.S73   1996
306'.0973—dc20   96–25473
                                                              CIP

Contents

Preface

The proposal to write this book originated with one of the authors, Peter McClelland. Without his initiative and his readiness and special competence to fill a critical gap (economics) in the range of disciplines required for the task, this book would not have seen the light of day. Once the project was undertaken, another set of circumstances helped to make it possible, for the concepts on which it is based, the form in which they are expressed, and the purpose for which they are used have a longer history.

These three elements were first systematically incorporated in an article published two decades ago in the *Proceedings of the American Philosophical Society* by another of the authors of this book, Urie Bronfenbrenner.[1] Entitled "Reality and Research in the Ecology of Human Development," the article, in its aim, form, and substance, was in effect a small-scale prototype of this book. That article was itself a product of convergent lines of basic research and field studies conducted from the late 1950s through the 1960s. The trends revealed by this work raised concerns about the future well-being of the nation's families and their children. In 1969, Bronfenbrenner expressed these concerns in invited testimony before the Committee on Ways and Means of the House of Representatives.[2] The following quotation captures the main thrust of the testimony:

Mr. Chairman, by profession I am a behavioral scientist. My field of specialization is human development, in particular the processes through which the newborn infant is gradually transformed into an effective member of society—in other words, the process of making human beings human.

As a specialist on that process, I am deeply troubled. The seriousness of my concern is perhaps best conveyed by an analogy. Suppose you were an astronomer studying the solar system and, as you examined your own scientific observations and those of your colleagues, you began to see some indications that the solar system was falling apart.

That is the situation in which I find myself. There is a growing body of scientific evidence that the process of making human beings human is breaking down in American society. The signs of this breakdown are seen in the growing rates of alienation, apathy, rebellion, delinquency, and violence we have observed in youth in this nation in recent decades. And the indications from the evidence are that these trends will be continuing at an increasing rate. The causes of this breakdown are, of course, manifold, but they all converge in their disruptive impact on the one institution that bears primary responsibility for socialization in our society—the American family. (pp. 1837–1838)

At that time, now a quarter of a century ago, such assertions were generally viewed with skepticism, or at most as an overstatement of the case. Today the problems described are all too familiar. Not only are they daily fare in the mass media, but more and more Americans are experiencing their effects, directly and indirectly, in their daily lives. If this is so, why should there be a special book on the subject, and why now? We can point to several reasons.

Most publications and media programs relating to this topic deal with one social problem at a time—for example, special reports focusing on family breakup, the decline in moral values and behavior, more crime in the streets, increasing numbers of families with young children in poverty, falling test scores, mounting youth violence and crime (resulting in ever greater numbers of youth in prison), outbreaks of racial conflict, the growing numbers of the aged requiring personal and medical care, and the soaring economic costs of dealing with these problems. Although these changes are treated separately, in fact all are related to each other.

In this book, for the first time, the demographic data on these trends are brought together and presented in such a way that the relationships among them can be recognized and systematically examined. The latter point is especially important. Not only are the facts about these phenomena usually presented separately, but they are often treated as if they were unrelated problems, each dealt with by its own experts and single-issue advocacy groups competing for the same limited public and private resources. As a result, it becomes difficult to ascertain the facts of the matter, to recognize the nature and power of the interdependencies, and to design, win support for, and carry out coordinated and cost-effective strategies for coping with these problems simultaneously.

The authors of this book are scientists from different disciplines (economics, psychology, human biology, sociology, education, and developmental science) experienced in and committed to applying the findings of cross-disciplinary research for understanding and dealing with the human problems of our time.

As we show, many of these disruptive trends had their origins in the 1960s and 1970s. By the 1980s, however, they began to escalate and reinforce each other, to the point where today they have reached a critical stage that is much more difficult to reverse. The main reason is that forces of disarray, increasingly being generated in the broader society, have been producing growing chaos in the lives of children and youth, not only in the home but also in other settings as young people move beyond the family into what are often disrupted and disruptive child care arrangements, classrooms, schools, peer groups, neighborhoods, and entire communities.

As we document in this book, a history of growing up in such environments has become one of the strongest predictors of the growing social problems confronting American society and of the accompanying decline in the competence of character of the next generation as we enter the twenty-first century.

Finally, although far broader in scope than its earlier prototype, this work intentionally omits a topic accorded a prominent place in its

1975 predecessor. The final section of that article was entitled "Implications for Public Policy" and recommended specific changes in major social institutions—"old ones modified, and new ones introduced—so as to rebuild and revitalize the social contexts that families and children require for their effective functioning and healthy growth."[3]

We offer no such recommendations here because we believe that proposing specific policy for reversing current disruptive trends in the lives of the nation's families and children would serve as yet another stimulus to divisiveness, and thus divert attention from our primary purpose: communicating as clearly and compellingly as we can the nature and gravity of the crisis confronting the nation as a whole, in the fervent hope that this will help to spur and sustain a common effort to alter our course toward increasing societal chaos, which threatens the future competence and character of this generation and the next.

1

YOUTH

Changing Beliefs and Behavior

There is no more critical indicator of the future of a society than the character, competence, and integrity of its youth. One of the major themes of this book is the increasing threat to the social, physical, and moral development of youth. This chapter examines trends over time in beliefs and behavior among teenagers that reflect character, competence, and integrity. We seek evidence as to whether a larger number of youth now evidence beliefs and behaviors indicative of poor adult adjustment than in the past and whether problematic beliefs and behaviors are confined primarily to poor, disadvantaged youth, or are more widely prevalent, even among more advantaged children.

FIGURE 1–1

TRUST IN OTHERS HAS DECLINED OVER TIME

U.S. High School Seniors

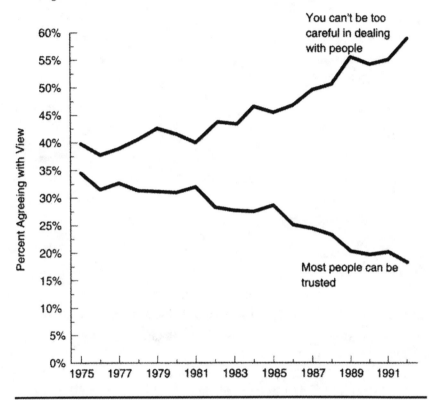

- Since 1981, a decreasing number of high school seniors have been reporting that "most people can be trusted." In 1981, 31% of students agreed with that statement, and 40% believed that "you can't be too careful dealing with people." By 1992, only 18% agreed that most people could be trusted, and 59% were endorsing the more skeptical response. What has happened?[1]

- As the next figures show, this growing mistrust of others across time is paralleled by changes in a number of beliefs and behaviors.

FIGURE 1–2

VOTING HAS DECLINED IN PRESIDENTIAL ELECTIONS

Voters, by Age, in the United States

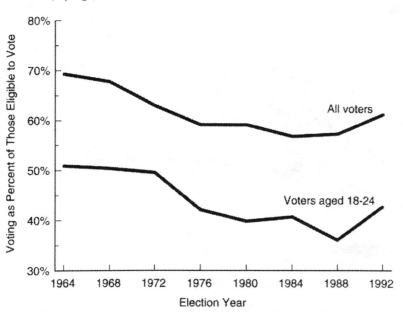

- Over successive new cohorts of youth, political participation has decreased. In 1964, 51% of eligible and registered voters aged 18–24 voted in the presidential election. In 1988, 36% of the registered in this age group voted. Although there was a rebound in voting in 1992, the percentage who voted (43%) was lower than in 1964.

- Clearly the trend in youth voting reflects the well-known national trend. The rate of decline in participation is about the same as for the registered electorate as a whole (compare to the upper line in the figure). In contrast, a larger proportion of the registered voters aged 65 and older voted in 1992 than in 1964. Only youth aged 18–24 reported a participation rate lower than 50%.

FIGURE 1–3

CHEATING AND TOLERANCE OF CHEATING HAS INCREASED OVER TIME

High School Students and College Students in Honor Code Colleges

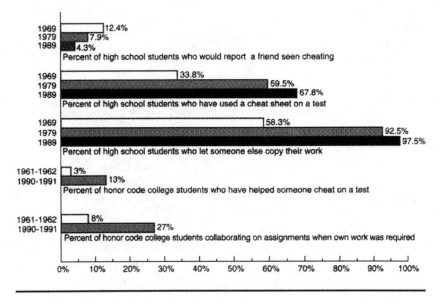

- More youth report cheating in school, as well as increased tolerance of cheating among their peers. Data from large samples of students in high school and college tell the story. Among high school students, the percentage of those who would report a friend seen cheating declined from 12% in 1969 to 4% in 1989, a proportion suggesting that peer regulation of cheating has disappeared. The percentage of high school students who report ever using a cheat sheet doubled, from 34% to 68%. Virtually every high school student in 1989 (97%) admits having let another student copy from his or her work.

- These beliefs and behaviors also have increased among college students. Honor codes—that is, peer enforcement and sanctioning—have not deterred an increase in cheating. At colleges with honor codes, the proportion of students who have helped someone cheat on a test has quadrupled since the 1960s, from 3% to 13%. At these same colleges, the number who have handed in work on which they have inappropriately consulted with other students has more than tripled, to 27%.

- Cheating is approximately twice as widespread at colleges that do not have honor codes but has increased at a somewhat lower rate. Taken together, the trends suggest that honor codes are becoming less of a deterrent because of students' greater tolerance of cheating.

FIGURE 1-4

TEENAGERS' TOLERANCE OF OUT-OF-WEDLOCK BIRTHS INCREASED IN THE 1980s

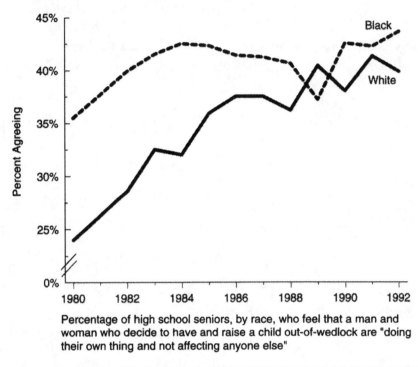

Percentage of high school seniors, by race, who feel that a man and woman who decide to have and raise a child out-of-wedlock are "doing their own thing and not affecting anyone else"

- In 1992, more than 40% of white and black high school seniors reported that a man and woman who have a child out of wedlock are "not affecting anyone else." This proportion has risen since 1980. Significantly, the increase in endorsing this belief is greater among white teenagers (24%, increasing to 40%) than among black teenagers (from 35% to 44%).

- The increasing tolerance co-occurs with the recent increase in births to unmarried teenagers (see Figure 4–11).

- The examples presented thus far, illustrating a range of behaviors and beliefs, point to the conclusion that today's youth adhere less to traditional norms of behavior and hold less traditional beliefs than youth did 30 years ago. Subsequent chapters in this book (chapters

2, 4, 5, and 6) will show that premarital sexual behavior, labor force participation, and some aspects of educational achievement are showing similarly nontraditional, even negative, trends. Together they suggest an increasing threat to the integrity, character, and competence of youth.

• What accounts for changes in the beliefs and behaviors of youth? One possibility is that youth are receiving less or less effective guidance from traditional, socializing institutions, such as their families or religion. Another possibility is that parents of teenagers (single parents, overworked parents) are not supervising them as closely as parents of previous generations did. The rising rate of poverty among children may also be implicated, through lack of opportunity, or increased exposure to physical threat and violence.

FIGURE 1–5

**WEEKLY RELIGIOUS ATTENDANCE HAS DECLINED
OVER TIME**

U.S. High School Seniors

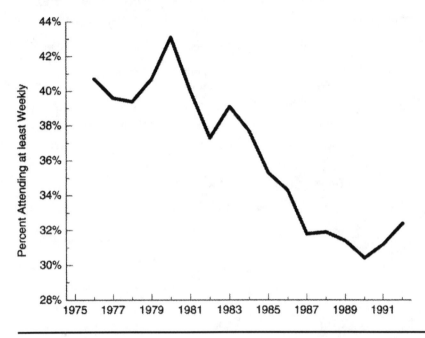

• Religious participation is in decline among youth. (There is, however, a recent increase.) Overall, 41% of all high school seniors in
1976 reported attending religious services at least weekly. In 1992,
about 32% attended weekly.

FIGURE 1–6

TEENAGERS' RELIGIOUS ATTENDANCE, BY FAMILY STRUCTURE

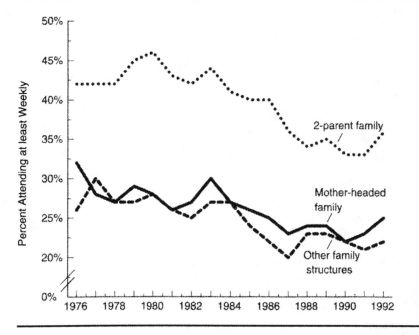

- The overall decline in youth weekly church attendance is roughly parallel across two-parent, mother-headed, and other family structures. Teenagers in two-parent families, however, are on average more likely to attend religious services weekly today than they were in the 1970s.

- The increasing proportion of teenagers being raised in mother-only and other nontraditional families over the time period covered by this figure may be associated with the overall decrease in weekly church attendance. Because a larger proportion of teenagers are being raised in nontraditional households and, on average, teenagers in nontraditional households are less likely to attend church weekly, the proportion of youth attending church weekly is declining.

- It is also clear that reported weekly church attendance has declined in two-parent families. Thus another possible explanation for the decline in weekly church attendance by youth is that their parents are less likely to attend religious services. Over this same period of time, adult weekly church attendance appears to have decreased as well.[2]

FIGURE 1-7

ATTITUDES TOWARD OUT-OF-WEDLOCK BIRTHS

By Religious Attendance and Race, U.S. High School Seniors

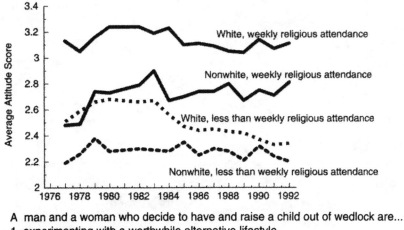

A man and a woman who decide to have and raise a child out of wedlock are...
1=experimenting with a worthwhile alternative lifestyle
2=doing their own thing and not affecting anyone else
3=living in a way that could be destructive to society
4=violating a basic principle of human morality

- Religious participation has implications for other beliefs. High school seniors who attend church weekly are less likely to believe that those who have and raise children out of wedlock are either "experimenting with a worthwhile alternative lifestyle" or "doing their own thing and not affecting anyone else."

- Overall, white youth are less likely than nonwhites to express moral tolerance of nonmarital pregnancies. From 1976 to 1992, however, nonwhites who attended church weekly became somewhat less morally tolerant (on average), while whites who do not attend church weekly became somewhat more tolerant.

FIGURE 1–8
ACHIEVING AN A GRADE-POINT AVERAGE
By Family Structure, U.S. High School Seniors, 1990–1992

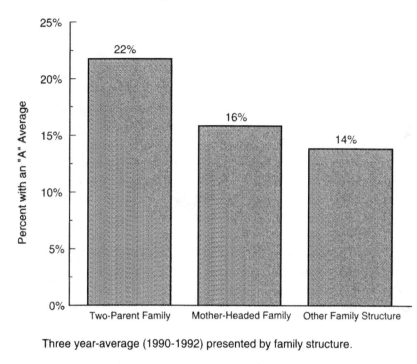

Three year-average (1990-1992) presented by family structure.

- Family structure is associated with another important indicator of future competence: how well one does in school. High school students in two-parent families are more likely to achieve A or A– averages than students being raised in mother-headed and other nontraditional family settings.

- Grade-point averages have implications not only for future plans (e.g., college) but also for current behavioral choices, including cheating, drug and alcohol use, and delinquency. The source for these data on grade-point average and family structure does not provide information about cheating, but other data sources show that teenagers with lower grade-point averages are more likely to cheat.[3] Possibly some of the reported increase in high school cheating is related to the increase in single-parent families and the shifts in beliefs and behaviors concomitant with not having both parents available—specifically less supervision of teenagers and more susceptibility to peer influence.

FIGURE 1–9

SKIPPING DAYS OF SCHOOL IN THE LAST FOUR WEEKS

By Family Structure, U.S. High School Seniors, 1990–1992

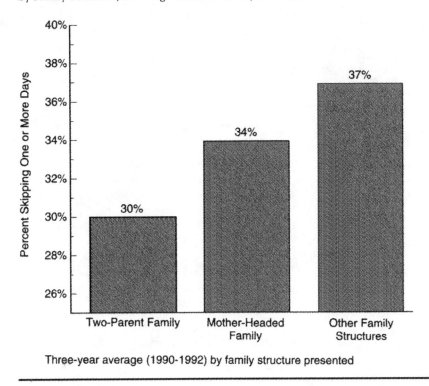

Three-year average (1990-1992) by family structure presented

• Consistent with the suggestion that high school students from non-traditional families may on average be less supervised by parents, high school seniors in nontraditional families are skipping classes somewhat more frequently than students from two-parent families. Skipping classes more frequently is associated with a lower grade-point average.

FIGURE 1–10

TEENAGERS' AVOIDANCE OF DRUG USE IS RELATED TO
FAMILY STRUCTURE

U.S. High School Seniors, 1990–1992

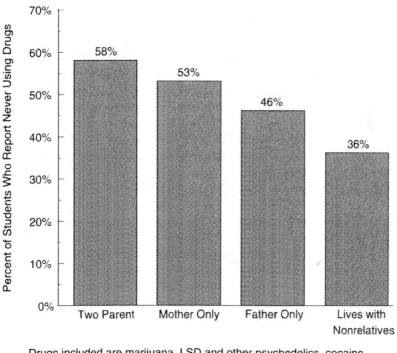

Drugs included are marijuana, LSD and other psychedelics, cocaine,
amphetamines, tranquilizers, barbiturates, heroin, and other
narcotics.

Three-year average (1990-1992) by family structure presented.

- Teenage drug use is also associated with family structure. In 1992, high school students in two-parent families are more likely to report that they have never used drugs (58%) than students from families headed by a single mother (53%) or a single father (46%). Teenagers being raised by nonrelatives, a living situation that may reflect serious family disruption in their past, are least likely to report being drug free (36%).

- The data source used here is the most-watched measure of youth drug use in the United States. Taking a broader view, these data indicate that high school student drug use is less prevalent now (36% reported using drugs in 1994) than in 1976 (when 45% reported using drugs). Drug use among students has increased since 1992, after a long decline. This overall pattern over time has special significance. Although an increasing number of teenagers were residing in nontraditional families through the 1980s, this living situation did not exacerbate the teenage drug problem. The investigators who collected these data have demonstrated that increasing use is related to availability of the drugs and perceived risk of harm. Availability has been increasing recently for some drugs, such as marijuana, and students on average are less likely to believe that using them will cause harm.[4]

• In other words, the campaign against drug use in the 1980s (which included both restriction of supply and education about the risks of drugs) worked in spite of the increasing prevalence of family situations that could have increased drug use. Binge drinking declined as well.[5]

FIGURE 1-11

TEENAGERS' AVOIDANCE OF DRUG USE IS RELATED TO RELIGIOUS ATTENDANCE

U.S. High School Seniors, 1990–1992

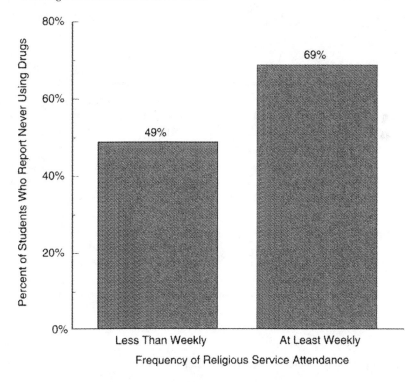

Drugs included are marijuana, LSD and other psychedelics, cocaine, amphetamines, tranquilizers, barbiturates, heroin, and other narcotics.

Three-year average (1990-1992) by family structure presented.

- Teenage drug use is also associated with church attendance. Over 1990–1992, 69% of high school seniors who attended church weekly were drug free, compared to 49% of those who attended less frequently.

- Taken together, the information presented in Figures 1–6 through 1–11 suggests that the future competence of some of today's teenagers might be enhanced if they were more integrated into traditional social institutions.

FIGURE 1–12

TEENAGERS' TRUST IN OTHERS IS RELATED TO FAMILY STRUCTURE

U.S. High School Seniors, 1990–1992

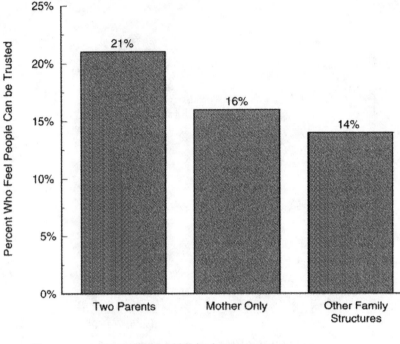

Three-year average (1990-1992) by family structure.

- Although it is possible that integration into traditional social institutions is related to a sense of trust (see Figure 1–1 and Figure 1–12) shows that while youth raised in two-parent families are more likely to think other people can be trusted (21%) than those from nontraditional families, the majority nevertheless believe that "you can't be too careful in dealing with people." Perhaps teenagers who feel that they have few committed family members on whom they can rely generalize this belief to include the trustworthiness of the world at large—or perhaps today's youth express less trust because they fear more for their futures and their physical safety.

FIGURE 1–13

TEENAGERS WHO DISAGREE WITH THE VIEW THAT PLANNING ONLY MAKES YOU UNHAPPY SINCE PLANS HARDLY EVER WORK OUT ANYWAY

U.S. High School Seniors

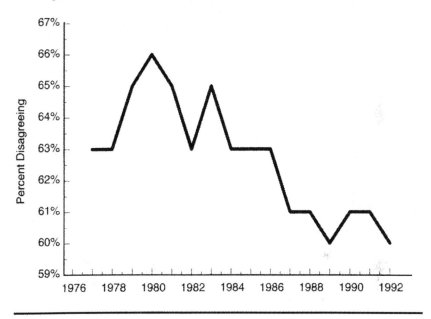

- Increasingly, high school seniors may be less optimistic about their future. In 1980, 66% of high school seniors disagreed with the statement, "Planning only makes you unhappy since plans hardly ever work out anyway." In 1992, 60% disagreed with that statement.

FIGURE 1–14

**TEENAGERS WHO DISAGREE WITH THE VIEW
THAT PLANNING ONLY MAKES YOU UNHAPPY
SINCE PLANS HARDLY EVER WORK OUT ANYWAY**

By Family Structure, U.S. High School Seniors

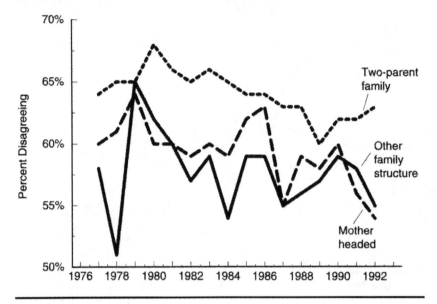

- Compared to 1980, faith in planning has declined for youth, regardless of family structure, although teenagers from two-parent families are more likely to have faith in planning. Since 1990, however, the gap between expectations has widened for youth from two-parent vs. other families. One possible explanation for the difference by family structure is that teenagers with absent parents foresee fewer opportunities to carry out plans.

FIGURE 1-15

**TEENAGERS WHO DISAGREE WITH THE VIEW
THAT PLANNING ONLY MAKES YOU UNHAPPY,
SINCE PLANS HARDLY EVER WORK OUT ANYWAY**

By Mother's Education, U.S. High School Seniors

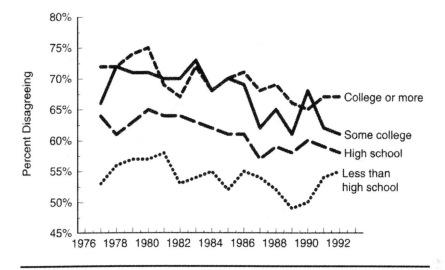

- If it is likely that youth raised by two parents have more opportunities than youth raised by only one parent, then faith in planning should be related to the family's economic prospects. This figure displays that faith in planning is strongly associated with one measure of current family income, mother's education.

- The information in this and previous figures shows that beliefs and behaviors reflecting diminished self-regulation and expectations for the future, as well as disregard of rules, are evident among a significant proportion of today's youth and in all reported family structures. As the number of children raised in nontraditional families increases as a proportion of all youth, as is now happening, such behaviors may rise if we do nothing to deter them. The record of teenage drug use over time shows that is it possible to deter such behaviors.

- The call for deterrence raises many issues, not the least of which is how deterrence can be accomplished. The fact that teenagers in two-parent families also report deviant behavior indicates that factors in the environment affect everyone. Teenagers themselves report that violence in their schools and neighborhoods, and the hopelessness they feel in defending themselves against it, is their biggest worry. The next figures portray the violence experienced by youth and their reactions to it.[6]

FIGURE 1–16

YOUTH ARE MORE LIKELY THAN ADULTS
TO BE VICTIMS OF VIOLENT CRIME

United States, 1993

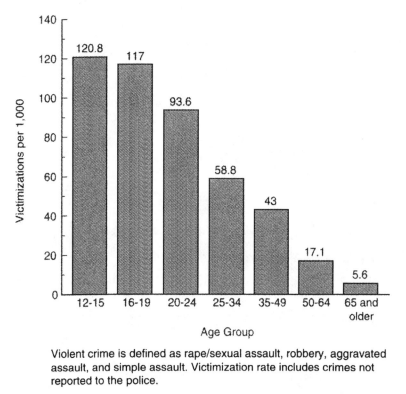

Violent crime is defined as rape/sexual assault, robbery, aggravated assault, and simple assault. Victimization rate includes crimes not reported to the police.

- Youth are at least five times more likely than adults age 50 and older to be victims of violent crime. The data in the figure, from a 1993 national survey of approximately 100,000 Americans in 50,000 households, show that youth are exposed to more violence than adults of any age. (For comparison to data on youth as sources of the violence, see Chapter 2.) These data, based on self-reported interviews, do not include a growing risk to youth: death by homicide. They do include the 60% of violent crimes that were not reported to the police.[7]

FIGURE 1–17

VIOLENT CRIME VICTIMIZATION RATES

By Race, Income, and Place of Residence, Persons Aged 12 and Over,
United States, 1993

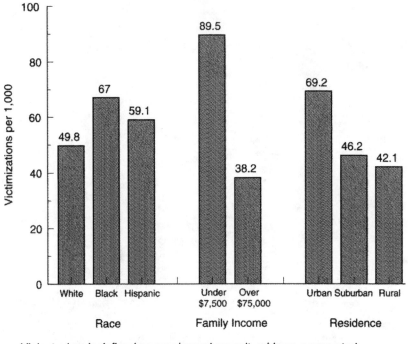

Violent crime is defined as rape/sexual assault, robbery, aggravated
assault, and simple assault. Victimization rate includes crimes not
reported to the police.

- Exposure to violence is not equally distributed across race, income level, and place of residence. Blacks and Hispanics, the poor, and urban dwellers are more likely to be victims of violent crime.

- Exposure to violence is not equally distributed across groups of youth. Young black males aged 12–24 experience violence at a rate greatly above that experienced by other age and racial groups. Black male teenagers aged 16–19 had twice the victimization rate of white males that age and three times that of white females aged 16–19. Young black males are more likely than young whites to be attacked by weapons— four times more likely to be attacked by someone using a handgun.[8]

FIGURE 1–18

VIOLENCE IN SCHOOLS

Teen Beliefs and Behaviors in the 1990s

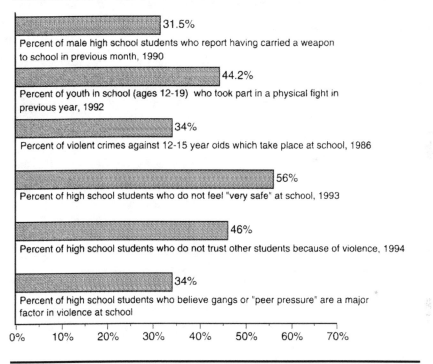

31.5%

Percent of male high school students who report having carried a weapon to school in previous month, 1990

44.2%

Percent of youth in school (ages 12-19) who took part in a physical fight in previous year, 1992

34%

Percent of violent crimes against 12-15 year olds which take place at school, 1986

56%

Percent of high school students who do not feel "very safe" at school, 1993

46%

Percent of high school students who do not trust other students because of violence, 1994

34%

Percent of high school students who believe gangs or "peer pressure" are a major factor in violence at school

0%   10%   20%   30%   40%   50%   60%   70%

- Some may argue that these violent crime statistics refer to street youth, yet, as every parent of a teenager knows, the border between the street and the school is probably more permeable than that. The data displayed in this figure, collected from three independent sources, suggest that the street and the school are not independent.

- The first bar shows that 31.5% of male and 8% of female high school students carried a gun, knife, or club to school in the month previous to this 1990 survey. (These data were collected by the Centers for Disease Control from a sample of about 12,000 students.) Many of these weapons are carried for defense. Forty-four percent of all students (females included) took part in a physical fight in 1992.

- Schools are not havens from crime. In 1986 (latest national data available), 34% of all violence against youth aged 12–15 took place at school. Another 20% took place on the way to school. It is no wonder fewer than half of students surveyed in 1993 felt "very safe" at school.

• As the last two bars of the graph illustrate, students fear their fellow students and attribute violence to gangs and peer pressure.

FIGURE 1–19

TEENAGERS REPORTING DELINQUENT BEHAVIOR,
DRUG AND ALCOHOL USE, AND SEXUAL ACTIVITY

Rochester, New York, Youth Aged 13–17, 1989

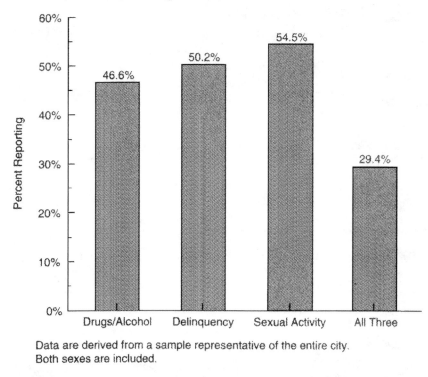

Data are derived from a sample representative of the entire city.
Both sexes are included.

- Gangs, delinquent behavior, and wide participation in other socially deviant behavior are not confined to the largest American cities. This figure shows that medium-sized cities—in this case, Rochester, New York—have a majority of teenagers involved in behavior that would have been much less common thirty years ago. Fifty percent of teenagers aged 13–17 in a representative sample of Rochester have committed a delinquent act, 47% have used drugs or alcohol, and 55% have had sexual intercourse. Twenty-nine percent have done all three. With behavioral deviance so widespread, the pressure from peers on younger, less experienced teenagers to participate is likely very strong.

FIGURE 1–20

PROFESSIONAL ETHICS IN THE 1990s

Beliefs and Behaviors of Lawyers and Medical Students

41%
Percent of California lawyers who believe the ethical standards of most lawyers are high, 1994

67%
Percent of California lawyers who believe attorneys are compromising professionalism as a result of economic pressure, 1994

22%
Percent of medical students who had personal knowledge of others cheating during examinations, 1991

19%
Percent of medical students who would permit another student to copy from them during an examination, 1991

12%
Percent of medical students who did not agree that failure to report an on-duty intoxicated physician is unethical

0%   10%   20%   30%   40%   50%   60%   70%   80%

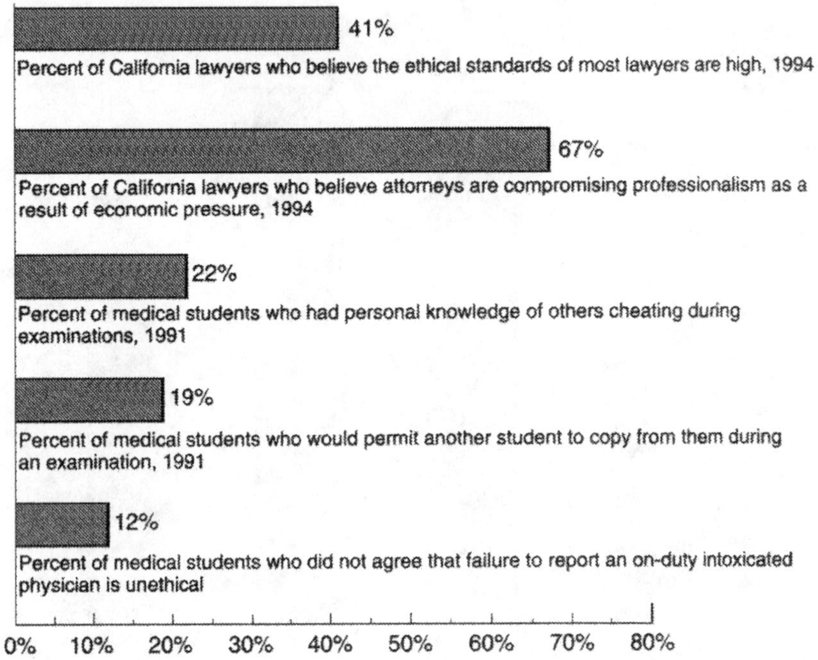

• These data, regarding the ethics of lawyers and medical students, show that the behavior of present and future professionals may already be compromised. Fifty-nine percent of California lawyers in a 1994 survey reported that the ethical standards of most lawyers were less than high. Sixty-seven percent of them believe that business and economic pressure are compromising legal professionalism. Forty-one percent of them (not reported in the figure) believe that things will only get worse.

• Cheating at medical schools may be almost as widespread as at undergraduate colleges. Although those admitted to medical schools must go through a rigorous screening process, 19% in this survey of one prestigious medical school would allow another student to copy from them on an exam.

• Ambivalence about self- and peer regulation is also evident among this sample. Twelve percent did not believe it is unethical to fail to report an on-duty intoxicated physician. In contrast, virtually all of their faculty—members of an older generation—did.[9]

LOOKING TO THE FUTURE

Youth, specifically teenagers, are more likely now than in the past to endorse beliefs that reflect lack of trust and withdrawal from participation in conventional institutions and rejection of social convention and responsibility. Behaviors indicative of youth's potential to develop competence, integrity, and character also echo these trends. Nevertheless, some problematic behaviors, most notably illicit drug use, can be deterred.

There are a number of worrisome trends in the beliefs and behaviors reported by teenagers. Some of these may be associated with the increase in the proportion of youth being raised in nontraditional families, others related to their assessment of their economic prospects and their exposure to violence. More and more teenagers, for good reasons, perceive their futures as uncertain and their peers as dangerous. People with these beliefs may feel that the world is out of their control, a perception that can discourage socially constructive behavior.

We highlight two examples from the chapter. One is that the relative deficit in youth's socially constructive behavior (such as voting in elections) will have an impact on our political system. Socially constructive behavior also includes, moreover, self- or peer regulation of deviant behaviors among teenagers. As the data on school cheating (and attitudes toward out-of-wedlock pregnancy) show, this sort of self- and peer regulation has eroded significantly.

Many possible implications for the future arise from the data presented in this chapter. We shall emphasize two. First, youth who feel that the world cannot be trusted may be more likely to meet violence with violence than rely on teachers, parents, police, or prosecutors to resolve their disputes. In the next chapter we examine the impact that violent youth are having on our society. Another implication is that youth with uncertain or ambivalent ideas about what constitutes socially constructive behavior or who are less willing to accept social responsibility for regulating others' behavior are less likely to bring strong character and competence to their chosen professions.

2

CRIME AND PUNISHMENT

The previous chapter documented beliefs and behaviors that seem to pose threats to the development of competence and character among today's youth. Although these negative trends are evident among all youth, some of those most dangerous to the health and development of the next generation are more prevalent among the disadvantaged.

In this chapter, we focus on the prevalence and social impact of violence committed by youth. A relatively small number of violent youth go on to commit multiple violent crimes in adulthood. The critical question is whether the proportion of youth who become violent and antisocial, and who are likely to follow criminal careers, has increased in recent years. Yet even if the proportion has remained constant, their violence now threatens a wider segment of society. This chapter addresses these important questions and explores the costs of violence to society.

FIGURE 2–1

VIOLENT CRIME AND THE STATE OF THE ECONOMY

United States, 1960–1995

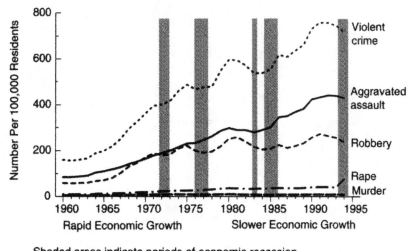

Shaded areas indicate periods of economic recession

• The rate of violent crime—defined by the Federal Bureau of Investigation and National Institutes of Justice as the reports of homicides, rapes, aggravated assaults, and robberies per 100,000 of the total population—has more than tripled since 1965.

• Reports of violent crimes were increasing during the period of rapid economic growth in the 1960s and 1970s, as well as during the more recent period of slower growth. In other words, the current rate of violent crime is not solely a product of worsening economic conditions for the nation as a whole in the past decade.

• Short-term spurts in violent crime reports do not necessarily correspond to recessionary periods. Sometimes violent crime reports increase during periods of recession (see 1973–1975), and sometimes they decrease (see 1981–1982). They have also spurted during periods of growth (see 1985–1986).

• The next figures suggest that social and historical development factors play a part in the high violent crime rate.

FIGURE 2–2

HOMICIDE DEATH RATES ACROSS TIME

Males Aged 15–24, in Canada, the United States, the Federal Republic of Germany, England and Wales, and Japan

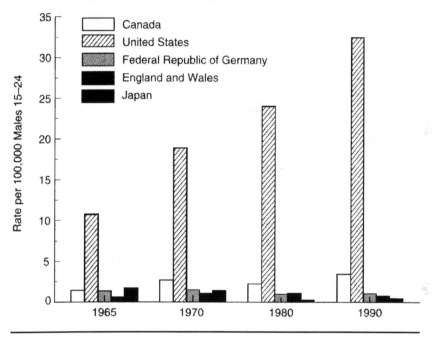

- The United States experiences significantly more violent crime than other world economic powers. Among violent crimes, homicide can be compared the most reliably across time and culture. Young men are the most frequent victims of homicide throughout the world. As the figure shows, the United States far outpaces other developed countries in the homicide deaths of young males; for example, the U.S. rate is ten times higher than Canada's.

- The United States, moreover, has experienced the largest increase in young male death by homicide among the five countries compared from 1965 to 1990. The sharpest contrast is with Japan, where the young male homicide death rate decreased from 1965 to 1990.

- Homicide is the second most frequent cause of death of males of this age group in the United States and the most frequent cause of death of black males of this age.[1]

FIGURE 2–3

U.S. WHITE FEMALE HOMICIDE AND U.S. NONFIREARM HOMICIDE RATES EXCEED OVERALL HOMICIDE RATES IN CANADA AND ENGLAND AND WALES, 1990–1992

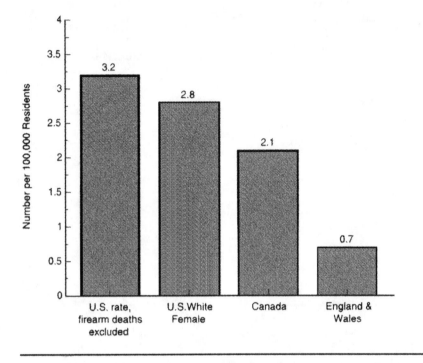

- It is tempting to conclude that the high rate of death by homicide in the United States is due to the high rate of homicide among black males. Certainly homicide is the leading cause of death among young black men, but the homicide rate for white women in the United States is higher than the total population homicide rates in Canada and England. (Women's homicide rates in Canada and England and Wales are less than one-third the rate for white women in the United States.) White women have a relatively low overall risk of homicide death in the United States—generally less than one-third that of white males and one-tenth that of of black males.

- Nor does the greater number of guns in private hands in the United States account fully for the higher homicide death rate. The U.S. homicide death rate by means other than firearms exceeds the total population homicide death rates in most other world economic powers.[2]

FIGURE 2–4

**PERCENTAGE INCREASE IN THE NUMBER
OF ARRESTS FOR HOMICIDE**

Perpetrators Under Age 18 and Perpetrators Age 18 and over,
United States, 1984–1993

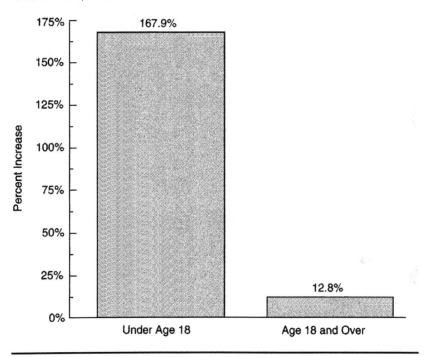

- Not only are the young more likely to be victims of homicide, they are more likely to commit it. From 1984 to 1993, the number of arrests for homicide increased 167.9% among youth under age 18. National data on arrest trends also show that youth account for a growing proportion of all arrests for homicide in the past decade. In 1984, youth younger than age 18 were 7.6% of all those arrested for murder. In 1993, less than a decade later, the percentage had more than doubled, to 16.4%.

- Youth violence is only part of the picture. Youth and young adults (aged 18–25) now account for the majority of those arrested for murder; 53% of all identified homicide perpetrators in 1993 were under the age of 25.

- The average age of those arrested for homicide in the United States declined from 32.5 years in 1965 to 27 years in 1993.

- Ninety-one percent of murderers under the age of 18 are male. More than half are nonwhite (53%). The rate at which black youth commit murder is about six times that of white youth and has increased more than three times as rapidly since 1984 (211%) as that of white youth (64%).[3] Greater involvement of black youth in the crack cocaine trade is believed to account for the racial difference in committing murder.[4]

FIGURE 2–5

INCARCERATION RATE

Five Developed Nations, 1990

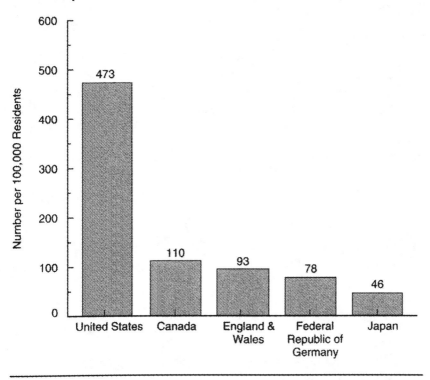

• The United States has a higher incarceration rate than other world economic powers, and it is higher by a wide margin: in 1990 (the latest date for which international rates can be compared), 473 per 100,000, or more than four times that of Canada and Great Britain.

FIGURE 2-6

NUMBER OF INMATES IN LOCAL JAILS, STATE PRISONS, AND FEDERAL PRISONS

Rate per 100,000 Residents in the United States, 1960–1995

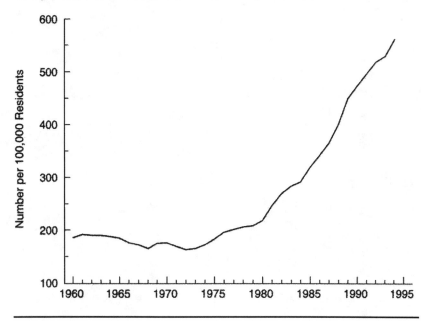

- The U.S. incarceration rate (persons imprisoned per 100,000 total population) has increased 204% since 1960 and 159% since 1980. The absolute number of prison and jail inmates has tripled since 1980, from about 500,000 to 1.6 million in mid-1995.

- In addition to the 1.6 million adults in jails or prisons at midyear 1995, it is estimated that at least another 3.75 million were on probation or parole.[5]

- The tripling of the number in prison or jail since 1980 is due to a number of factors, reflecting crime control measures as well as the overall crime rate. First, the overall and violent crime rates remained high throughout this period. Second, as a crime deterrence measure, more drug offenders involved with crack cocaine have been sent to prison. (From 1980 to 1994, the percentage of inmates in state prisons who were serving terms for drug offenses rose from

8% to 26%.) Third, many sentenced for violent crimes are remaining in prison longer. (Specifically, violent offenders served, on average, 42% of their sentences in 1992, 46% in 1994.) Since 60% of released prisoners are rearrested within three years (according to a 1989 federal study), longer sentences are being enforced as a way to keep violent criminals from committing more crimes.[6]

- The high rate of incarceration has economic and social consequences for the United States. Some of these are explored in the next several figures.

FIGURE 2–7

INCARCERATION RATES IN U.S. STATE AND FEDERAL PRISONS, BY RACE, ETHNICITY, AND SEX, 1980–1993

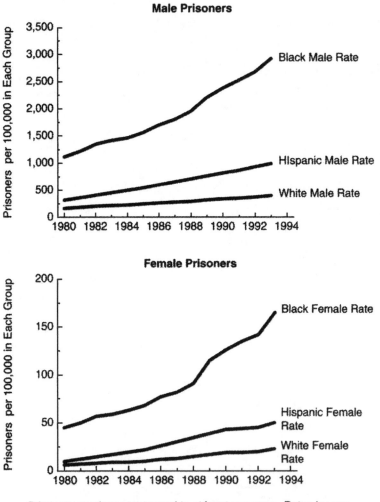

Prisoners are those sentenced to at least one year . Rates by sex and race are calculated using estimates of the U.S. population as of July 1 of that year. Hispanics can be either black or white.

- While black males constitute the majority of those sentenced to at least one year in prison, the rate of imprisonment is also rising rapidly among whites, Hispanics, and women. The absolute number of black males sentenced to more than one year rose 217% from 1980 to 1993, compared with 163% for white males. As these charts make clear, however, the rate of imprisonment has been increasing very quickly among other groups as well since 1980. The absolute number imprisoned is up 327% for white women, 343% for black women, and 449% for Hispanics.

• Approximately 6.8% of the adult black male population was in prison or jail at midyear 1995, compared to less than 1% of adult white males. The proportion of adult black men imprisoned has risen throughout this century—from 1% in 1920, to 1.7% in 1950, to 2.1% in 1980. The most rapid increase has been since 1980.[7]

• Incarceration rates differ significantly by age and education. The highest rate of incarceration is for black men aged 25–29: in 1990, 9% were in jail or prison. Black men (and white men) with less than a high school education were twice as likely to be incarcerated as other men: 16% of black men and 4% of white men with less than a high school education were estimated to be in jail or prison in 1990.[8]

• One explanation for the racial disparity is that crime is an alternative source of income for those who face employment discrimination. Others would argue that involvement in crime reduces the chances of being employed, either because crime promises greater short-term financial gain than employment or because convicted criminals are less likely to be hired for jobs. The next figures address some of these issues.

FIGURE 2–8

MALE LABOR FORCE PARTICIPATION BY RACE

Age Groups 16–19 and 20+, 1960–1993

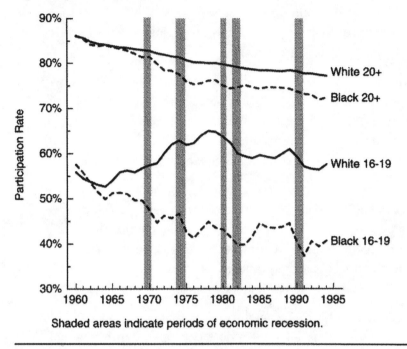

Shaded areas indicate periods of economic recession.

• The labor force participation of black male teenagers has been declining since 1960, in marked contrast to white male teenagers, whose participation has held roughly steady. (Participation rates of adult men, black and white, have fallen at roughly the same rate.) These trends are consistent with the suggestions that young black men are more involved in crime because they lack access to legitimate employment, perceive greater financial opportunity through crime, or become less desirable as employees through criminal involvement. At a minimum, it suggests that many young black teenagers are only tenuously connected to the legitimate labor market.

• There is considerable evidence that drug selling supplements earnings from legitimate jobs in America's inner cities. A recent 1990 study of residents in two impoverished inner-city neighborhoods found that 49% to 66% of the work-age men under age 45 were involved in drug selling, as were 27% to 44% of the women. Those who sold drugs reported incomes at least 300% higher than non-sellers identified in those neighborhoods.[9]

• The relative size of income that can be generated from drug selling is very large in comparison to the size of income from the type of legitimate work inner-city black males are likely to find.

FIGURE 2–9

EMPLOYMENT VERSUS CRIME AFTER INCARCERATION

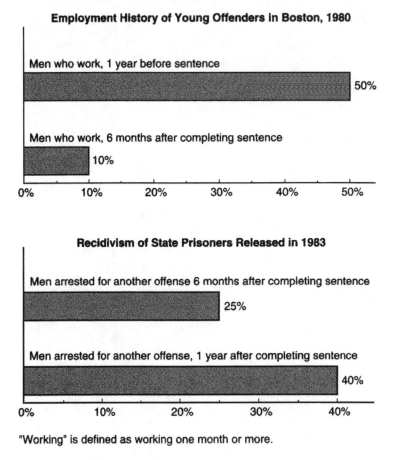

Employment History of Young Offenders in Boston, 1980

Men who work, 1 year before sentence
50%

Men who work, 6 months after completing sentence
10%

0%   10%   20%   30%   40%   50%

Recidivism of State Prisoners Released in 1983

Men arrested for another offense 6 months after completing sentence
25%

Men arrested for another offense, 1 year after completing sentence
40%

0%   10%   20%   30%   40%

"Working" is defined as working one month or more.

- A conviction record is related to subsequent employment among young men. The employment rate falls dramatically for those sentenced to jail. These data are derived from a study of young men in high-unemployment areas.

- The recidivism rate (committing another crime after serving a sentence) is very high. The bottom figure suggests that the short-term recidivism rate may be higher than the postincarceration employment rate. These data, derived from a national study of half of all state prisoners released in 1983, also show that released prisoners who were younger or who had attained less education (groups more comparable to those whose experiences are summarized in the top two bars of this figure) were more likely to commit another crime than average.[10]

- There are two ways to explain these data: that released criminals have difficulty finding employment or that those sentenced to prisons have a strong propensity to engage in further crime, a propensity existing prior to their sentence.

FIGURE 2–10

GOVERNMENT EXPENDITURES FOR JUSTICE AND CORRECTIONS, CORRECTED FOR INFLATION, 1971–1990

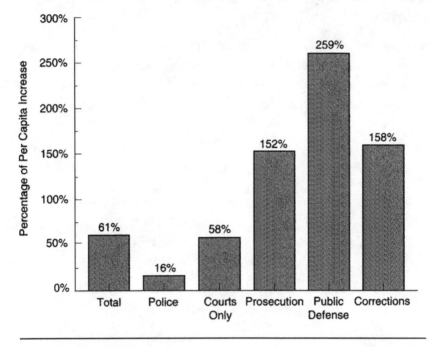

- Dealing with the increasing rate of crime has been very costly. Overall, justice and correction costs, corrected for inflation, have risen 61% per capita since 1970.

- The increase in the number of reported crimes has caused court and corrections-related expenditures to increase the most; expenditures on police protection have increased the least.

- In 1992, the American states spent $20.2 billion on prisons, representing 3.3% of total state general expenditures. In 1970, state expenditures on prisons were 1.4% of total state general expenditures.[11]

- In 1992, U.S. counties and municipalities spent $10.3 billion on local jails. In 1993, the average operating cost per inmate in a local jail was $14,667. (On average, local jurisdictions spent an additional 22% constructing and improving jail facilities.)[12]

• There are other rising costs of crime and crime control for businesses and individuals in addition to their impact on taxes, including the 1.5 million private security and police officers in the United States, some of whom are filling gaps in protection available from public services.[13]

FIGURE 2–11

RELATIVE EXPENDITURES ON CORRECTIONS AND HIGHER EDUCATION

Four States and U.S. State Average, 1965–1966 and 1991–1992

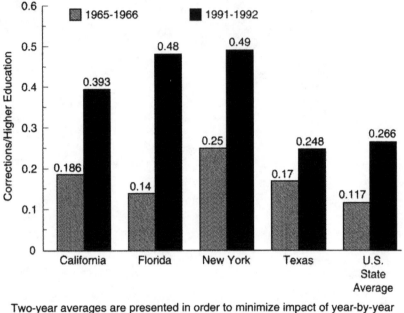

Two-year averages are presented in order to minimize impact of year-by-year variations brought about by elections, political change, and economic trends.

- In four states with high crime rates, large prison populations, and demand to build more high-security prisons (California, Florida, New York, and Texas), state expenditures on corrections have increased faster than state expenditures for higher education since 1965–1966. For example, in 1965–1966, California spent 18.6 cents on prisons for every $1 it spent on universities and colleges. In 1991–1992, it spent 39.3 cents on prisons for every $1 on higher education. Historically these four states have been committed to maintaining large, prestigious state-supported university systems, at relatively low cost to their citizens. They are also not atypical: in the average state, the ratio of corrections expenditures to higher education expenditures has increased 127%.[14]

- This trend over time, combined with the continued high rate of violent crime and longer sentences, suggests that prison expenditures may overtake higher education expenditures in several states. In 1995, California spent an equal percentage of its state budget on corrections and higher education: 9.8% toward each. In 1965–1966, California directed 3.5% of its budget toward corrections and 20.7% toward higher education.[15]

- Expenditures for crime control and prisons have strong support. Since 1980, a large majority (79–86%) of surveyed Americans have reported that the courts do not deal harshly enough with criminals. In 1994, 75% reported that "too little" was being spent on "halting the rising crime rate."[16]

- Other branches of government as well as public opinion are driving increases in expenditures for corrections. In 1992, a quarter of 503 large jurisdictions were under court order to relieve crowding in their jails. One response has been to build more jail cells. State and federal prisons face the same crowding pressures.[17]

FIGURE 2–12

VIOLENT CRIMES COMMITTED BY YOUTH WILL DOUBLE BY 2010

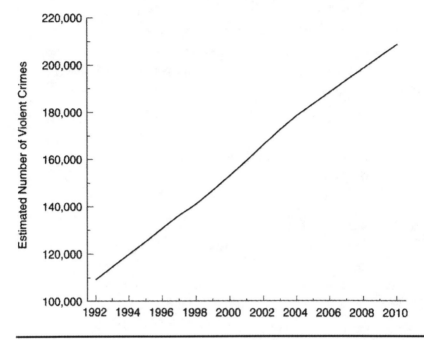

- Reports of violent crime have decreased somewhat over the past four years (see Figure 2–1); homicides, for example, have declined. Yet population projections suggest that violent crime will begin rising again by 1997 as the number of young men aged 10–17 in the population increases. Crimes committed by youth are projected to soar as their numbers increase in the population if no new measures are in place to deter them. The data presented here are projections based on the assumption that crimes perpetrated by youth will continue to increase at the same average rate they increased during the past ten years. (Each year, for every 100,000 youth, there will be a 2.8% increase in the *rate* of crimes committed.)[180]

- Expenditures will have to keep pace with this threat, by both expanding the current justice and corrections system and developing new deterrence measures.

LOOKING TO THE FUTURE

The data presented here on crime rates and government expenditures necessary to deal with crime are of critical importance. Violent crime and its effects are no longer as confined to the larger cities and poorer neighborhoods. Moreover, the increasing proportion of crime committed by youth, the growing dominance of black men in prison and crime, and the changing racial composition of the population suggest (other things being equal) a continuing increase in crime and incarceration, and their related expenses. If real wages for the least skilled continue to fall, the economic appeal of crime may grow as well. A lack of belief in the American dream and a growing sense of desperation among the less educated could foster shorter time horizons, which may lead more of them to discount the losses and dangers associated with crime and incarceration in favor of short-term gain.

The data presented in this chapter have important implications for those who will be dependent on family members or government transfer programs for their financial support. The rising rate of youth criminal involvement, and its potential to reduce the potential lifetime earnings of many young men, is an issue that deserves scrutiny and attention.

Young men are those whose wages have traditionally supported children. Their earnings are a major source of tax revenue, and thus a major contributor to government transfer payments to those who are necessarily dependent because of youth, old age, or disability. In 1993, the number of men aged 16–34 in jail or prison was equal to 3.1% of men that age in the labor force (153,729 young men). Assuming an average income of $18,737 (the average high school graduate income in 1994), this represents a loss of $2.9 million in earnings for one year. The social security taxes lost from this sum are $386 million. This figure, for one year alone, does not include the proportion of wages "lost" by those who are convicted of crimes and return to the labor force with reduced earning potential.

We do not propose that prison be abolished. Thousands who are imprisoned are a danger to innocent citizens, and their crimes cost the economy billions of dollars in years of lives lost to random murder, security and protection costs, and theft and casualty losses that individuals and businesses must absorb. In 1992, the National Institutes of Justice estimated that the total economic loss from crime was $17.7 billion.[19] However, the rising crime and incarceration rates among the poorest of our population are in themselves direct threats to the ability of other individuals in those groups who hope to establish their own households, raise children, and support their elderly. The criminologist Jerome Miller predicts that as many as 50% of adult black men under the age of 40 will be incarcerated in the year 2010.[20] James Alan Fox, another criminologist, finds this prediction alarmist and suggests that the proportion will be lower. Yet even if the actual proportion in jail or prison is 25%, this is a large enough reduction of the adult black male population to drive the marriage rate still lower and reduce average income among the poor (in constant dollars) still more.

Broader social implications are also troubling to contemplate. If present trends continue, the average economic prospects of black men would almost certainly worsen. Crime, despite its risks, might attract still more men—and women. The potential for racial conflict over issues of crime and punishment in the next generation should not be discounted.

3

ECONOMIC DEVELOPMENTS

The hopes and aspirations roughly captured by the phrase "the American dream" have long included two major economic goals: to realize, through a lifetime of work, a rising standard of living between initial employment and final retirement and to provide for one's children in such a way that they will be better educated, earn more, and live better lives than their parents. Many Americans believe that the chances of achieving both are in decline. A 1995 poll, for example, found that of the parents surveyed, only half expected their children to be better off than they were, two-thirds believed that the American dream was becoming more difficult to achieve, and three-quarters expected those difficulties to intensify in the years immediately ahead (see Figure 3–1).

These perceptions of waning economic possibilities are supported to a disturbing degree by actual economic developments of recent decades. Arguably the most important economic trend in the United States since the early 1970s has been the marked slowdown in the growth of productivity and the related slowdown in the growth of output. If gross national product (or gross domestic product) is analogous to a pie, the pie has been growing since 1973 at an average annual rate far below that recorded in the 1950s and 1960s. Although the causes

FIGURE 3–1

AMERICAN ATTITUDES AND THE AMERICAN DREAM

1995 Survey of Parents

(1)	Do you expect your children will have a better life than you have had, a worse life, or a life about as good as yours?	Better life . . . . 46% Worse life . . . . 20% About as good . . . . 27% No children . . . . 6% Not sure 1%
(2)	For most Americans, do you think the American dream of equal opportunity, personal freedom, and social mobility has become easier or harder to achieve in the past 10 years?	Easier to achieve . . . . 31% Harder to achieve . . . . 67% Not sure 2%
(3)	And do you think this American dream will be easier or harder to achieve in the next 10 years?	Easier to achieve . . . . 22% Harder to achieve . . . . 74% Not sure 4%

of this slowdown are poorly understood, the main effects are clear. If productivity growth slows, then the growth of real wages (or wages corrected for inflation) must also slow, as must the family incomes of those whose major sources of income are earnings in the labor market.[1] If output per person grows at 2.5% per year—which it did between 1948 and 1973—then the average standard of living of Americans should double in less than thirty years. Alternatively, if output per person grows at only 1.2% per year—which it has done since 1973—then the average standard of living will take twice as long to double. In fact, real median family income has hardly grown at all since 1973, while the trends in average real wages, measured in various ways, have either leveled off, or declined. At the same time, sources of income going disproportionately to higher-income groups, such as interest, profits, dividends, and capital gains, have tended to register significant gains.

As the growth of the pie has slowed down, the division of the slices has become more unequal. During the era of rapid economic growth in the immediate postwar decades, all income groups, from the wealthy to the poor, recorded significant advances. Since 1973, the rich have become richer, and the very rich have gained the most, while the poor have become poorer in both relative and absolute terms as their real wages and real incomes have fallen significantly. The earnings of the least skilled have declined, widening the gap in entry-level wages paid to those with, and without, a college education. Last, but of first importance to the least advantaged, the lower the family income, the lower the odds of going to college and finishing college.

The implications of such trends for all but the wealthiest of Americans would seem to be that the economic aspirations embedded in the American dream must be significantly scaled back. For that minority in this country least capable of protecting itself—the children of the poor—the implications are grimmer. The number of children raised in poor families has been rising. Whether their parents are working or on welfare, the real family income of the least well off has been falling. Not surprisingly, the opportunities for upward economic mobility available to those at the bottom are widely perceived as being in decline, as the growing fashionability of the term *underclass* makes clear. At the heart of these diminished opportunities is one causal sequence apparent to all: if family income significantly affects the child's chances for more and better education, and if the amount of education is a crucial determinant of future earnings, the falling real incomes of the least advantaged suggest that the American dream is in danger not of fading but of disappearing altogether for many children.

FIGURE 3–2

TOTAL GROWTH IN OUTPUT PER MAN-HOUR
1955–1973 and 1974–1992

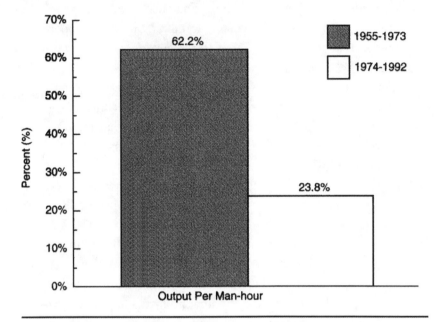

- If the question made fashionable by former New York mayor Ed Koch—How am I doing?—is directed to any economy, the most fashionable answer focuses on a single measure: output per man-hour. The numerator commonly consists of some estimate of the total goods and services produced during a given year (such as gross domestic product, or GDP), and the denominator is the sum total of hours worked by the nation's labor force during the same year.[2] Dividing the first by the second gives output per man-hour. The growth in this measure over time is one indication—and a good indication—of how productivity is improving (once the "output" in the numerator is corrected for inflation, or for changes in the general price level).[3]

- If this productivity measure is used to assess how well the American economy has been doing, the answer is: Not very well, of late. Productivity growth has slowed dramatically since the early 1970s, from 62.2% to 23.8%.[4]

• If the growth of output slows, the growth of income of those paid to create that output is also sure to slow. This is particularly true for labor. About 70% of family income is earned in labor markets. (The remaining payments take such forms as profits, interest, and rent.) The trends in Figure 3–2 thus create the expectation that the growth rate in the average wage paid to American workers will also have slowed in the past two decades.

FIGURE 3–3

WAGES IN THE UNITED STATES

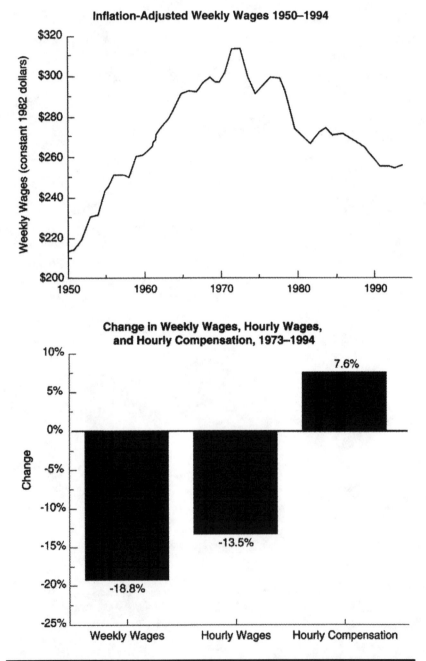

Inflation-Adjusted Weekly Wages 1950–1994

Change in Weekly Wages, Hourly Wages, and Hourly Compensation, 1973–1994

- The expectation of slower growth in the average wage paid understates the negative forces actually at work in American labor markets. Weekly wages corrected for inflation have fallen back to levels not seen since the late 1950s.[5]

- Optimists attack the point that payments to labor have fallen sharply by arguing that the measure is wrong. The trend in weekly wages, they claim, overstates the decline. The fall in hourly wages is much less. The main reason for the difference is the reduction in the average number of hours worked per week. Moreover, the optimists continue, a third measure of payments to labor—hourly compensation, which includes wages and fringe benefits—has actually risen in the past two decades. This rise in hourly compensation reflects a marked upward trend in fringe benefits in the past two decades, particularly the explosion in costs associated with health care. But if the focus is shifted from what employers have to pay for workers to the dollars actually received by those who work, then attention must shift away from the third measure (hourly compensation) and back to the first (weekly wages). By the first measure, inflation-adjusted wages have declined markedly since the early 1970s.[6]

FIGURE 3–4

MEDIAN FAMILY INCOME IN THE UNITED STATES

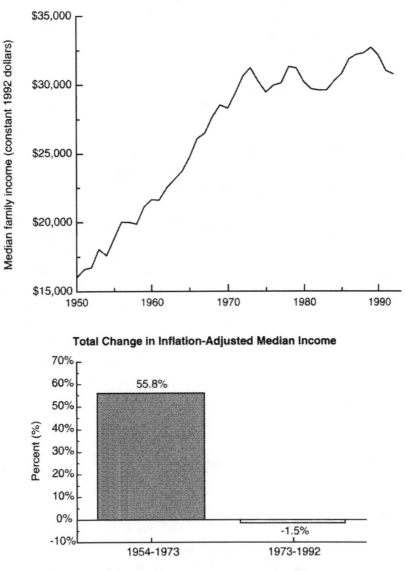

• If real wages, or wages corrected for inflation, are growing slowly or even falling, the same is likely to be true of family income, particularly in families whose primary sources of income are earnings in the labor market. This inference must be qualified to take account of two powerful influences on the trends in American family incomes particularly in evidence during recent decades. The first, boosting family receipts, is the rise of the two-earner family as progressively more women with families enter the labor force. The second, working in the opposite direction, is the rise of single-parent families that are headed, to an overwhelming degree, by women with low skills and limited earning power. The combined effect of these and other influences on the average family income in America is depicted in Figure 3–4.[7] After rapid advances in the 1950s and 1960s, the upward trend slowed dramatically and has remained sluggish ever since. The magnitude of this slowdown is better illustrated by a comparison of the total growth achieved in two nineteen-year periods, 1954–1973 and 1973–1992.

• The changing pattern since 1973 in the aggregate economic measures examined to this point—a dramatic slowdown in productivity growth accompanied by a sharp decline in average weekly wages and negligible growth in average family income—has been accompanied by a growing sense among a growing number of Americans that their long-run economic prospects have taken a turn for the worse. The director of the University of Michigan consumer surveys recently reported, for example, that for the first time in fifty years, these surveys are revealing a decline in expectations, with uncertainty and anxiety increasing as people look farther into the future.

• Once again, the optimists have a counterargument, which is a variant of their argument about wage trends. Look at a different measure, they suggest, and a different pattern emerges. While average family income has been relatively stagnant, they point out that the average size of families has been going down. (The average household size has fallen by 14% in twenty years, from 3.01 persons in 1973 to 2.63 in 1993.) The same income allocated to fewer people implies that the minor growth in total family income translates into a slightly larger growth in income per family member.[8] More important, they continue, if attention is shifted from family income to per capita personal income, the latter has registered a relatively robust growth per year since 1973 (on the average, about 1.4%).[9] The implication is that, on the average, those living in family units have fared less well than adults not living in family units. In fact, between 1967 and 1992, the real median income of married couples rose by 30% if both adults worked but by just 3% if only one adult worked. Moreover, in the same twenty-five-year period, the median income of families with no children rose by 36%, while families with one or two children did less than half that well, and families with three children experienced almost no gain. "In short: the more your household looked like a traditional family, the worse it fared economically in the period since 1967."[10]

• All of these measures of average income (family and per capita) tend to mask trends in income distribution that bode ill for the realization of the American dream by large numbers of Americans. Among those numbers are two groups whose chances for advancement are clearly going down: the children of the poor, whose likely economic fate is appropriately gauged by the trend in family income, particularly the family incomes of the least advantaged, and the group of adults at the bottom of the economic ladder whose limited skills and limited incomes impair their access to higher rungs. No amount of statistical juggling or quibbling about appropriate measures of aggregate economic performance can obscure two disturbing trends: the poor are getting poorer, and the number of children living in poverty is on the rise.

FIGURE 3–5

GROWTH OF FAMILY INCOME

Quintiles and Top 5%

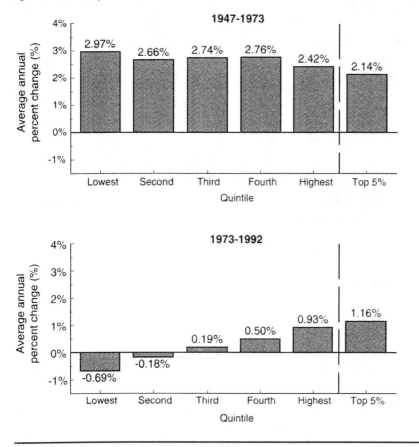

- The discussion now shifts from measures of aggregate growth to questions of how the benefits of growth have been distributed—or in terms of the pie imagery used previously, our focus at this juncture is not the growth of the pie but the size of slices received by different income groups within America.

- Imagine all people in this country organized into five income groups of equal size and then the groups aligned from those in the highest income quintile to those in the lowest. How the inflation-adjusted income of each group grew over time is illustrated in Figure 3–5. ("Top 5%" is merely the upper end of the top quintile.)

• The early 1970s appear to be an important turning point in the post-war era. Prior to that time, the performance of the economy was consistent with a metaphor made popular by President Kennedy: a rising tide lifts all boats. Aggregate growth was on the rise, and the lift it gave to the family incomes of all income groups is clear. Indeed, the highest annual income growth rates were recorded by the lowest quintile, which meant that the poor were becoming less poor in both relative and absolute terms. Beginning about 1973, however, this pattern changed. Growth slowed, and income distribution began to become more unequal. The rich continued to get richer, although their annual gains were, on the average, well below those recorded in the decades prior to 1973. More ominously, the incomes of the poor began to decline.

FIGURE 3–6

INFLATION-ADJUSTED WAGE GROWTH

By Wage Percentile, 1979–1989

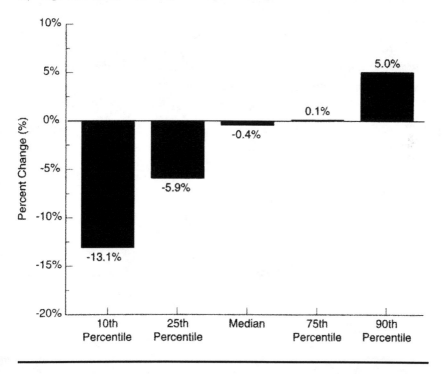

- This same general pattern—the top groups gaining and the bottom groups losing—is also evident in wage data since 1979. The divisions in Figure 3–6 have been changed, from quintiles to percentiles, but the overall trend has not.[11] As was true of family income, the wages of those at the bottom have been falling in recent years, while the wages of those at the top have continued to rise.

- According to a recent Census Bureau study, the gap between rich and poor in the United States is the widest it has been since that government agency began monitoring income distribution trends in 1947.

- These recent trends in inflation-adjusted wages understate the growing economic difficulties of the lowest paid because their recorded wages do not reflect their reduced access to health and pension benefits. In the decade ending in 1989, for example, pension coverage for the lowest fifth of wage earners in the private sector fell by almost half (from 18% to about 13%). In 1992, less than 40% of those who did not graduate from high school had company- or union-provided health insurance.

• These are new and uncharted waters for the American economy. Since 1929, when the data were first collected, the United States has never before experienced a combination of a sustained rise in real GDP per capita and a persistent decline in real wages for the majority of its workforce.

FIGURE 3–7

INFLATION-ADJUSTED ANNUAL WELFARE BENEFITS

For Mother and Two Children, 1975–1992

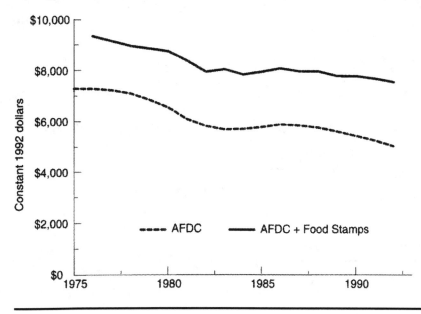

• While the incomes of the least skilled and lowest paid have been falling because their wages have been dropping, the incomes of those on welfare have also been falling because of a marked decline in the inflation-adjusted value of the average benefit paid out by the two major welfare programs in this country: food stamps and Aid to Families with Dependent Children (AFDC). Since the mid-1970s, a sharp drop in average AFDC benefits combined with a slight rise in food stamp payments has resulted in a net decline of roughly 20% in the inflation-adjusted value of the two programs combined.

FIGURE 3–8

PERCENTAGE OF AMERICANS LIVING IN POVERTY
By Age, 1960–1993

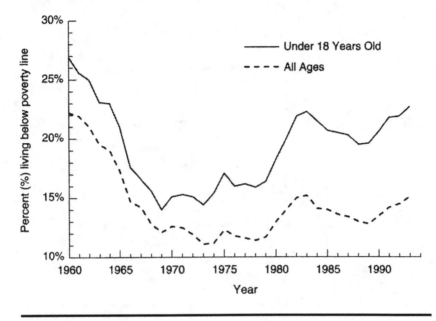

- The two quite different downward trends in wages paid to the least skilled workers and in means-tested payments to those on welfare have meant that the least well-off in America have become worse off in the past two decades. Not surprisingly, the number of those officially classified as poor has been going up.[12] The percentage of those living below the poverty line has been on the rise since the early 1970s.

- The age group hardest hit has been children. Between 1977 and 1993, for example, the poverty rate for working families with children rose from 7.7% to 11.4%. Compared with the poverty rate of all ages, the rate for those under 18 has been rising faster and by the 1990s had reached levels more than twice as high as the poverty rate for adults. At present, roughly two of every five Americans officially classified as poor are children. (More analysis of these developments is provided in Chapter 5.)

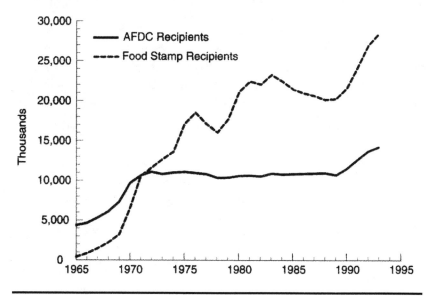

FIGURE 3-9
RECIPIENTS OF WELFARE AND FOOD STAMPS
1965-1993

- The long-term upward trend in poverty since the mid-1970s should be distinguished from short-term swings in that trend largely attributable to short-lived recessions, such as those that occurred in the early 1980s and the early 1990s. These momentary downturns in the economy appear to have a decided (if unsurprising) effect on measured poverty and the numbers receiving food stamps, but their impact on the number of AFDC recipients has been much more muted.

- Other evidence can be marshaled to support the contention that inequality is on the rise within America. Some of it is anecdotal. For example, the compensation of corporate chairmen, on the average, was 35 times that of a typical worker in 1980. By 1990, it was 135 times as great. (According to a 1994 survey of 424 large corporations, the average compensation of a chief executive officer was $3.7 million.) Another example is that women in the top earnings quintile since 1973 have gained, in inflation-adjusted dollars, 30 times as much as women in the bottom quintile. Estimates of other aggregate trends point in the same direction. Estimates of wealth held by Americans, for example, indicate a growing concentration in recent decades, although these data are more tentative than income or wage data, and the purported trends in wealth are thus more controversial.[13]

• Americans by and large have never been preoccupied with income inequalities as such, or evidenced much interest in policies whose sole purpose was to lessen income inequality by redistributing income. What has been a widely shared concern from the founding of the republic to the present has been the kind of inequality that impairs the opportunities to better one's condition through personal effort. From this perspective, the question raised by all of the previous numerical series (and not yet addressed) is whether slowing growth and rising income inequality are indicative of developments impairing the opportunity of those at the bottom of the economic ladder to reach for higher rungs. If that has happened, what has become imperiled, particularly for the least advantaged, is nothing less than the American dream.

FIGURE 3–10

PERCENTAGE OF THOSE WITHIN A GIVEN INCOME QUINTILE WHO EXPERIENCED GAINS OR LOSSES

1970s versus 1980s

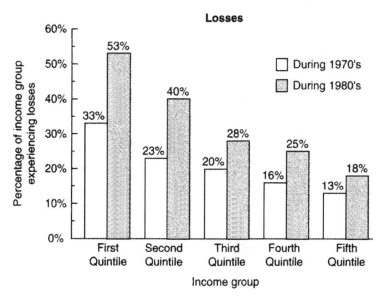

Losses

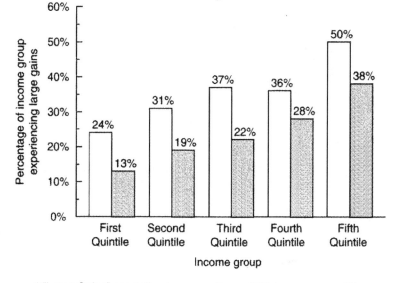

Large Gains*

* "Large Gains" are defined as more than a 70% increase over 10 years.

• We have come then, finally, to a question of fact easy to pose but difficult to answer. In recent decades, have the chances of upward mobility gone down, particularly for those at the bottom of the economic ladder? Direct evidence is difficult to find. One type of indirect evidence bearing on this question is the percentage of all individuals within a given income quintile who have experienced "losses" or "large gains," defined somewhat arbitrarily as more than a 70% increase in income over ten years.[14]

• Compared to the 1970s, the number in each quintile experiencing losses in the 1980s rose significantly, with the largest increase in losers experienced by the lower quintiles. There is a related pattern for those experiencing large gains. As the percentage of losers in all quintiles rose between the 1970s and the 1980s, so the percentage of winners in each quintile fell. But even with this decline, the basic tendency across quintiles remained: the higher the income group, the larger the percentage of those experiencing large gains. These data suggest that over the past few decades, the odds of experiencing losses have been highest, and the odds of experiencing large gains have been lowest, for those in the lowest income quintile, and those odds for this bottom group have become significantly worse in recent years.

FIGURE 3-11

DROPOUT RATE

By Family Income and Race, 1993

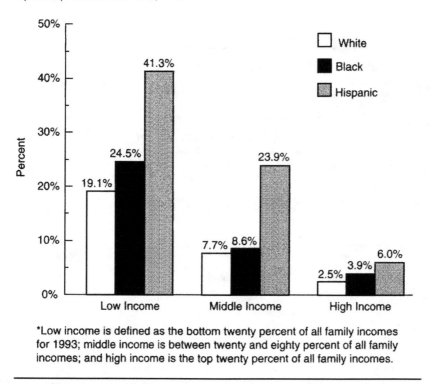

*Low income is defined as the bottom twenty percent of all family incomes for 1993; middle income is between twenty and eighty percent of all family incomes; and high income is the top twenty percent of all family incomes.

- These changing odds relate to adult income by income group. A related question is whether, if parents receive less income, the odds of their children's receiving a good education go down. Here, too, available evidence can only suggest aggregate tendencies by income group.

- The high school dropout rate of those in the lowest income group (irrespective of race) is more than six times the dropout rate of those in the highest income group.

FIGURE 3–12

AVERAGE S.A.T. SCORES

By Income Level, 1994

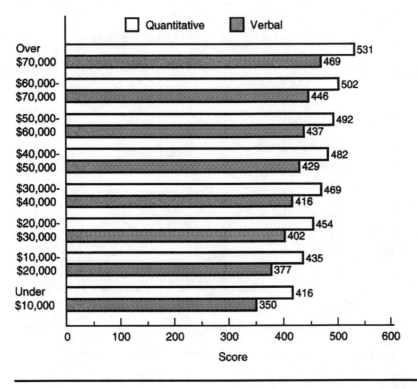

- Children from families earning more than $70,000 a year, on the average, score over 100 points higher on Standard Achievement Tests (SATs) than do children from families who earn less than $10,000 a year.

FIGURE 3–13

COLLEGE ENROLLMENT AND GRADUATION RATES

By Income Quintile, 1975–1984

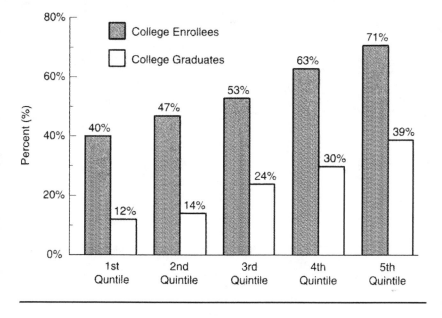

- Roughly three out of every four children whose family is in the highest income quintile continue on to college, compared to two out of every five children from families in the lowest quintile. Similarly, the odds of graduating from college rise significantly, the higher the family income of the student.[15]

- As the relative cost of attending college has been going up, the financial aid available to low-income families has been going down. The average cost of attending college has risen by over one-third since 1980, but tuition grants for low-income students are now less readily available. In the 1970s, for example, more students received need-based grants from the federal government than the number who borrowed under federal student loan programs. Now borrowers outnumber grant recipients by a wide margin.

FIGURE 3–14

ENTRY LEVEL INFLATION-ADJUSTED WAGES

By Educational Attainment, 1973, 1979, 1988

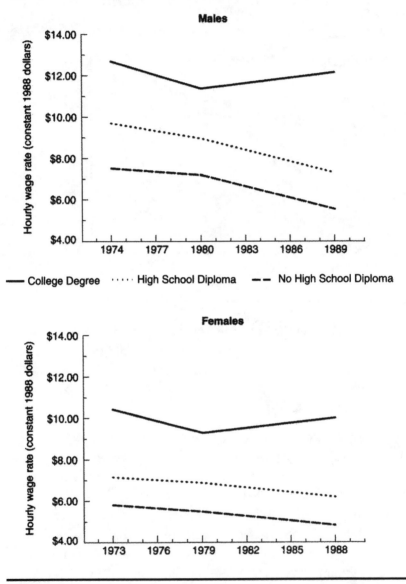

- As one would expect, the chances to earn more go up with a better education. The extent to which the relative rewards for increased education have risen in recent years is dramatic. Since 1973 inflation-adjusted wages have been falling for new entrants into the labor market, irrespective of the amount of education received. But entry-level wages for college graduates have fallen the least, creating a widening gap between the initial earnings of those with a college degree and those without.

FIGURE 3–15

INCREASE IN BENEFITS OF HIGHER EDUCATION

Based on Ratios of Median Income for Various Education Levels, 1974–1990,

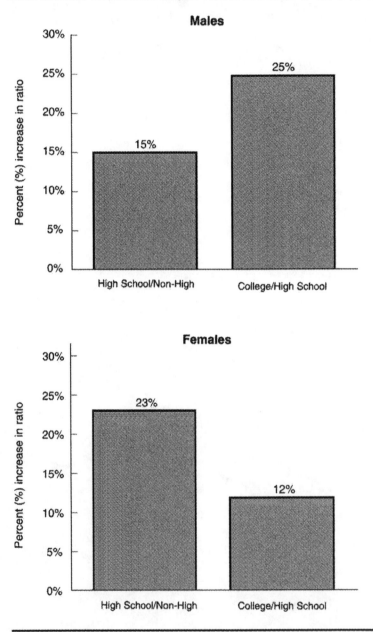

• The relative gains in earnings by the more educated are clear. For both men and women, those with high school diplomas have done better, on the average, than those without, and those with college degrees have done better still. (The percentages in Figure 3–15 indicate the advance in the average income of one group relative to another with less education but do not preclude a decline in wages overall.)

FIGURE 3–16

EMPLOYMENT GROWTH AND UNEMPLOYMENT RATES IN SELECTED COUNTRIES

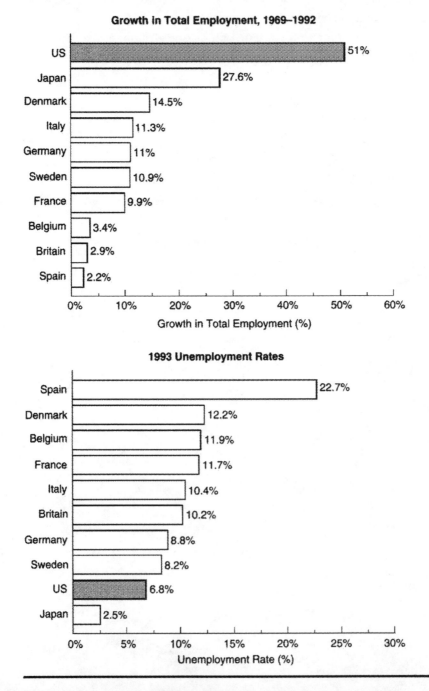

Growth in Total Employment, 1969–1992

Country	Growth
US	51%
Japan	27.6%
Denmark	14.5%
Italy	11.3%
Germany	11%
Sweden	10.9%
France	9.9%
Belgium	3.4%
Britain	2.9%
Spain	2.2%

Growth in Total Employment (%)

1993 Unemployment Rates

Country	Rate
Spain	22.7%
Denmark	12.2%
Belgium	11.9%
France	11.7%
Italy	10.4%
Britain	10.2%
Germany	8.8%
Sweden	8.2%
US	6.8%
Japan	2.5%

Unemployment Rate (%)

• The optimists want to shift attention to other measures of economic performance. They concede that the recent trend in wages has been somewhat disquieting, but they point to the fact that the American economy during the past quarter-century has excelled at job creation, at least when judged by developments in other industrial countries. Since 1969, for example, more new jobs have been created in the United States than in any other advanced industrial nation, and by a wide margin. Exceptional job creation has been accompanied, in recent years, by exceptionally low unemployment, with American unemployment rates well below those recorded in most European countries.

• These two achievements of high job creation and relatively low unemployment, runs a fashionable argument, are not unrelated to the rising inequality in America. European labor markets, compared with those in the United States, are riddled with rigidities. In the United States, less powerful trade unions and less generous benefits for those not working have helped create greater flexibility in labor markets. But when demand slumps, greater flexibility translates into lower wages. And one distinctive feature of the American economy in the past two decades is the extent to which wage inequality has increased and the wages of the least skilled have declined. From 1972 to 1990, for example, the United States experienced the largest increase in wage inequality of any developed nation. When the American economy rebounded from a recession in the early 1990s, roughly 2 million new jobs were created each year, but a large percentage of these offered wages below $8 an hour (or about $16,000 a year), with few if any health benefits and not much opportunity for advancement.

• Why this startling rise in wage inequality occurred in the United States is still a topic of debate. Some single out as particularly important a rising (relative) demand for skilled versus unskilled labor largely generated by improvements in technology, but probably reinforced by declining union strength, immigration, and increased global competition for products created by those who are the least skilled among American workers.[16]

- Whatever the reasons for rising wage inequality in the United States, what seems beyond dispute is that the working poor are getting poorer, the number of children living in poverty is on the rise, and the odds of these children receiving a good education are going down, as are their chances of gaining access to lucrative jobs with good opportunities for advancement.

- Will help be forthcoming from the two most obvious sources: new programs initiated by the federal government, or a rebound in economic growth that, as a rising tide, will again lift all boats? The most probable answer in both cases is not encouraging.

FIGURE 3-17

INFLATION-ADJUSTED FEDERAL BUDGET DEFICITS

By Administration, 1964–1994

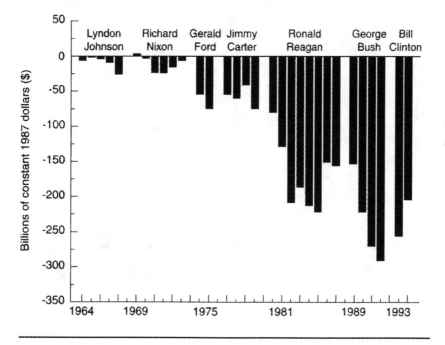

• Since the mid-1970s, as growth slowed and inequality increased, the federal government began to adopt fiscal measures quite without precedent in the peacetime history of the United States. Just when fiscal responsibility first vanished from the halls of Congress is far from clear, but by the 1980s irresponsibility was unmistakably in vogue and on display in the deficits exhibited by the above figure. The proximate cause is easily identified: spending increased while revenues remained about the same. As a percentage of GDP, federal expenditures rose, while receipts remained at roughly 18% to 19% of GDP.[18]

FIGURE 3–18

INCREASES IN INFLATION-ADJUSTED
GOVERNMENT WELFARE EXPENDITURES
1975–1991

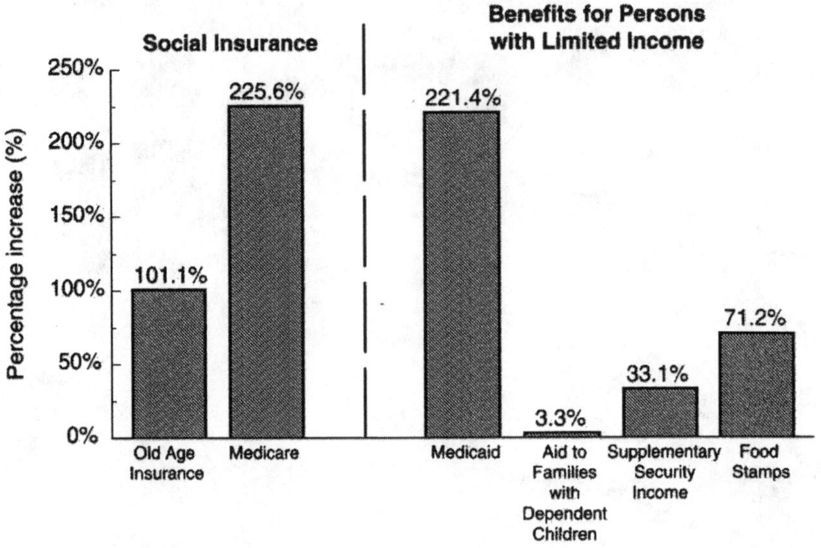

- Perhaps somewhat unexpectedly, the surge in government spending has been largely unrelated to the much-publicized War on Poverty. Indeed, if firepower is proportional to dollars spent, this particular war was little more than a skirmish. To be sure, Medicaid and Medicare expenditures shot up as spiraling health costs far outpaced the rate of increase in the general price level. This exception aside, however, the increases in federal spending targeted for the poor have risen very little in the past two decades.

FIGURE 3–19

FEDERAL OUTLAYS BY FUNCTION

Fiscal 1995

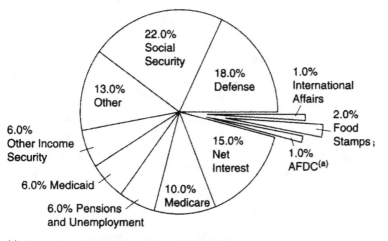

(a) Aid to Families with Dependent Children.

• The absence of large increases in past spending for the poor can also be detected in the present structure of federal expenditure patterns. Although Medicaid now constitutes 6% of total spending, food stamps and AFDC combined constitute only 3%. One implication is that whatever programs are initiated under the mantle of welfare reform in the immediate future, any associated cuts in means-tested benefits cannot be expected to make a major contribution toward deficit reduction. The benefits in question are too small relative to reductions needed to produce a balanced federal budget.

LOOKING TO THE FUTURE

This chapter began not with issues of government deficits or income inequality and the specter of fading opportunities, but by focusing on aggregate growth. The statement made there, and repeated here, is that arguably the most important economic trend in the United States since the early 1970s has been the marked slowdown in the growth of productivity and the related slowdown in the growth of output. For two centuries, the key to raising living standards and reducing poverty in the United States and expanding opportunities for its citizens has been a sustained rise in output per capita—an economic accomplishment that had never been achieved by any other nation at the time of the founding of this republic. If economic problems abound today and the federal government is mired in difficulties of deficit reduction, the most likely remedy for rising poverty and shrinking opportunities is the one that has worked so well throughout the nation's history, and particularly in the decades immediately following World War II: a surge in productivity, signaled by a significant and sustained rise in output per worker.

If output per worker is to rise, the most likely developments producing that result are the following:

1. An improvement in the quality of the workforce (in terms of skills and education).

2. An increase in the amount of cooperating factors of production per worker (a worker with a shovel can move more dirt than one without).

3. Improvements in technology (dirt moved per person per hour can be radically improved by the invention of a bulldozer).

What is the evidence that any or all of these may improve significantly in the immediate future?

Much has been written about the falling savings rate in the United States and how this decline bodes ill for trends in investment. The linkage to output per worker is fairly straightforward. The smaller the savings rate (other things being equal), the higher the price of borrowed funds, and thus the lower the incentive to invest, where "invest" here means not buying stocks and bonds but using borrowed dollars to acquire capital equipment (in economists' jargon "produced means of production"), such as bigger plants or better assembly lines. The less the annual investment (in this sense), the lower the addition to the nation's capital stock, and thus, on the average, each worker will have less capital to work with. And less capital per worker restricts the possibility for growth in output per worker.

But has this undesirable sequence been triggered in the recent past by a decline in the rate of saving?

As illustrated in Figure 3–20, gross saving (as a percentage of GDP) has fallen significantly in the past two decades, primarily because personal saving has declined and the public sector (mainly the federal government) has been running up large annual deficits (or has been dissaving). More meaningful—and more ominous—is the trend in net saving, or gross saving minus depreciation, because this is a better measure of net additions to the nation's capital stock. Net saving in America (as a percentage of GDP) has been falling continuously since the 1960s, although very recently it has shown a slight rise (see Figure 3–21). But even the most recent American saving rates are well below those of other leading industrial nations.[19] If this gap persists, eventually their labor force, compared to ours, will be working with more capital per worker.[20]

As savings trends of the recent past suggest, a surge in the amount of investment by Americans is unlikely in the immediate future, so developments in American education and labor markets suggest that a surge in the quality of the workforce is also unlikely in the coming years. That some quality improvement will be needed has become a commonplace, in part because more and better skills are being demanded in a workplace constantly modified by new technologies, including those involving more sophisticated information systems. Evidence abounds that many American workers are seriously deficient not only in advanced skills but in basic skills, such as the ability to read and write and perform simple arithmetical calculations. In 1995,

FIGURE 3-20
COMPONENTS OF GROSS SAVING
United States, 1960–1994

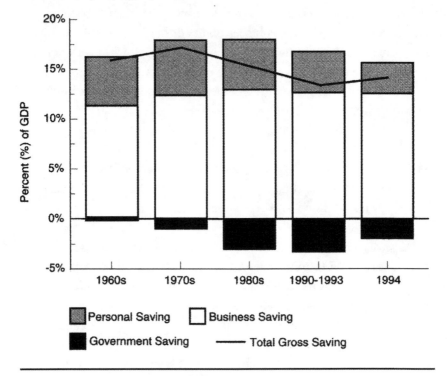

for example, the first national survey ever conducted by the Census Bureau of hiring, training, and management practices in this country found a striking lack of confidence among employers concerning the capacity of American schools *and colleges* to train young people for the workplace. Multiple instances of employer difficulties can easily be found, suggesting such dissatisfaction is not without justification; for example, New York Telephone had to test 60,000 applicants in order to find 3,000 with the skills needed for entry-level jobs, and Chemical Bank of New York has learned that it must test about 40 applicants to find one with the capacity to be a bank teller.

If the problem, at bottom, is defective education and job training, the most obvious solution is to improve the education system and expand job training programs. Neither seems likely to occur on a signifi-

FIGURE 3–21

GROSS SAVING, DEPRECIATION, AND NET SAVING

United States, 1960–1994

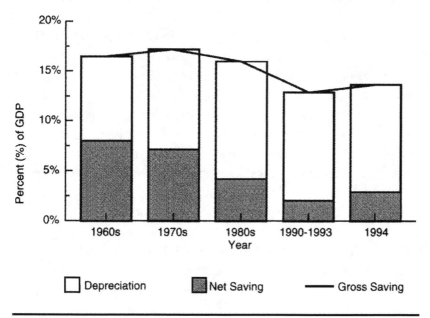

cant scale in the immediate future. Many public schools are losing progressively more teaching time in the wake of rising discipline problems and in-school violence. What teaching time there is has been subjected to the increasing demands of added programs, including those designed to combat a growing spate of problems associated with the shattering transformation of the American family. Large infusions of government funds are not likely to counteract these and other difficulties in an era of fiscal austerity. Indeed, that austerity will almost surely bring in its wake significant reductions in programs designed to aid the education process, such as remedial education, job training, and college grants and loans. Current demographic trends make clear that in the immediate future, the racial mix of new entrants into the labor force will feature fewer whites and more blacks and Hispanics, the latter two historically possessing on the average less education and fewer skills than their white counterparts. One final tendency likely to affect American labor markets in the years ahead—difficult to assess but possibly of the first importance—is a shift in attitudes and values among today's youth that may have adverse effects on success in school and later in the workplace. (These changes were explored in Chapter 1.)

One possibility remains: If in the near future output per worker is unlikely to be raised significantly by a sharp rise in investment (thereby increasing the supply of capital per worker) or by a major improvement in the quality of the labor force, it still might be raised by technological change. But here too the United States may be lagging behind other developed nations, although the evidence is more sketchy and less reliable than that for saving rates. American spending on nondefense research and development, as a percentage of GDP, has shown no significant change in the past two decades, while in West Germany and Japan such expenditure (as a percentage of GDP) has risen markedly.[21] Indeed, Japan now appears to be the world's biggest spender on civilian research and development. Nor are America's lagging research expenditures likely to be dramatically reversed by large infusions of federal funds in the immediate future, given Washington's preoccupation with deficit reduction.[22] The implications for this country's competitive position in a global economy are not encouraging. A number of other leading industrial nations are saving and investing at rates well above those in the United States, implying that their labor force will be working with more capital per worker than ours over time. Many of these same countries seem more successful at educating and training their workers (see Chapter 6). If they also outperform the United States in their rates of technological advance, the economic preeminence of this nation is sure to decline markedly in the not-so-distant future. Our main concern, however, has not been global competitiveness but domestic growth (although the two are not unrelated).

The problems that have taken center stage in this chapter are growing inequality, falling incomes for the poor, and the rising number of American children raised in poverty. The question is whether that classic restorative for so many economic ills—a significant and sustained rise in output per worker—can be expected in the near future to alleviate these particular economic ills. The answer depends on whether any or all of the three main causes of rising productivity can be expected to provide a significant boost to the American economy in the next decade. The odds that this will happen, however, appear to be discouragingly low.[23]

4

AMERICAN FAMILIES

Today and Tomorrow

In the preceding chapter, Peter McClelland graphically demonstrated the profound impact of economic conditions on the state of
Americans in general, and in particular the reduced ability of increasing numbers of Americans to realize the economic promise of the
American dream of a better life for themselves and their children.

Powerful as these economic changes are, there are also other forces at
work, as the first two chapters of this book documented. In Chapter 1,
Tara L. White and Elaine Wethington's findings of growing cynicism in
the beliefs and behaviors of high school and college youth revealed no
evidence that either long- or short-term economic changes were related to this general trend. They did discover, however, that there
were consistent differences in the family structures in which the youth
were raised, with those growing up in single-parent families being
more susceptible to developmentally disruptive influences. A similar
pattern emerged in Chapter 2, documenting the rising rate of crime
and violence in the lives of the nation's youth.

In this chapter, we focus directly on the profound structural
changes that have been taking place in American family life, the
groups most affected by these changes, and their consequences for the
development of the young. We are fortunate to be able to draw on the

multigenerational research design of the National Longitudinal Survey of Youth (NLSY), a study of over 12,000 youths, 14–22 years old, first interviewed in 1979 and reinterviewed every year since. The diverse data collected for this large sample make possible analyses of the enduring effects of childhood family structure and other family characteristics into the young adult years. The appendix at the end of this chapter describes the sample employed for the study and the nature of the information available.

We begin by documenting the structural changes that have been taking place in American families from the perspective of both space and time. Wherever possible we look first at these changes from an international perspective and then examine their evolution and distribution in different segments of the society. We then draw principally on data from the NLSY to analyze the impact of changing family forms on the subsequent development of young adults who have grown up in increasingly more different and disparate American worlds.

FIGURE 4–1

SINGLE PARENTHOOD IN DEVELOPED NATIONS

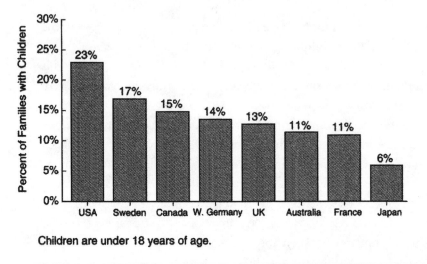

Children are under 18 years of age.

• The United States leads the modern world in adopting so-called new family forms: single-parent families, including those resulting from divorce.

FIGURE 4–2

DIVORCE IN DEVELOPED NATIONS

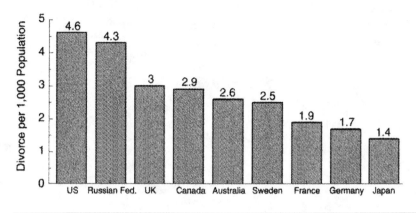

- This process is not a stable, steady state but a complex phenomenon taking place at a changing rate, with old forms becoming less numerically dominant as new forms take over.

FIGURE 4–3

**FEWER FIRST MARRIAGES AND FEWER BIRTHS
IN TWO-PARENT FAMILIES**

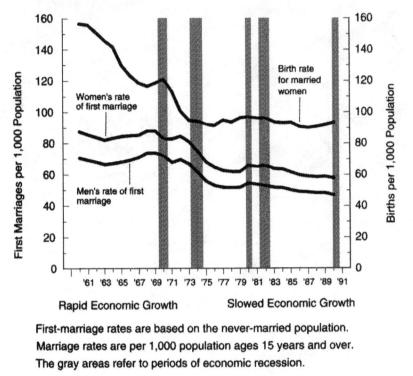

First-marriage rates are based on the never-married population.
Marriage rates are per 1,000 population ages 15 years and over.
The gray areas refer to periods of economic recession.

- In the late 1950s, the overwhelming majority of young children (95%) were growing up with two married parents. Today that proportion has dropped to less than 60%.

- One of the main reasons is a sharply falling rate of first marriage for both men and women. Another reason is that those who do marry are less likely to have children.

- Although responsive to short-term periods of economic recession, both marriage rates and birth rates to married women declined during the period of rapid economic growth. The shifting patterns point to the operation of other powerful forces besides the changes in the economy.

- The rate of first marriage is consistently higher for women than for men. This difference reflects the higher proportion of men who remain unmarried.[1]

FIGURE 4-4

REMARRIAGE RATES AFTER DIVORCE ARE ALSO FALLING

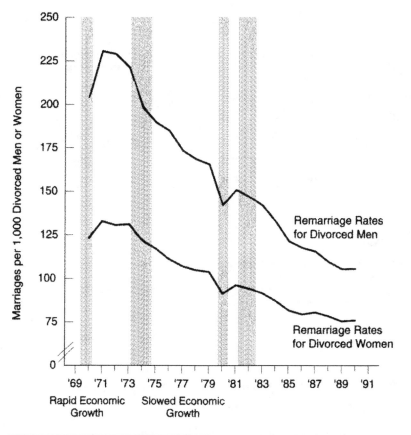

- The sharp decline over the past two decades in remarriage rates among the divorced further reduces the possibility that children will grow up in a home with two parents.

- In contrast to the data on first marriages, remarriage rates for divorced men are higher than those for divorced women. Because the decline is more rapid for divorced men, the gap between the genders is narrowing.

FIGURE 4–5

SINGLE PARENTHOOD FOR WHOM?

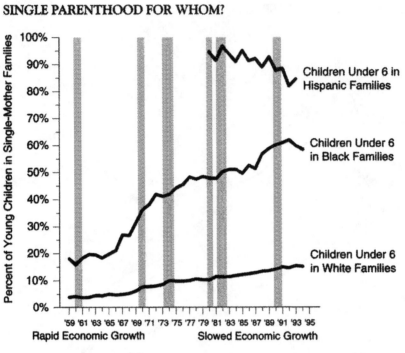

- The graph answers its own question. The steady increase in the number of young children growing up with only one parent has been occurring primarily in black families but also in white households.

- The situation for Hispanic youngsters presents a paradox. Systematic data first became available only in 1980. Although the percentage of young Hispanic children living with a single parent is by far the highest among the three ethnic groups, the rates have been declining.

- A complicating factor is that, in the language of the U.S. Census, Hispanics may be of any race.[2] In fact, most of them are also counted as either white or black. As of 1994, of the 17.1 million children in the United States under 6 years of age, 80% were white and 16% black. Split between them were 2.3 million children classified as Hispanics and constituting 15% of the total population under age 6. Whereas over the past decade the proportion of young white and black children in the population has remained relatively stable, the percentage of Hispanic youngsters increased from 9% in 1984 to 15% in 1994.

- Information on the percentage of single parents with young children in black families and white families has been available over a much longer period, and the trends over time reveal marked differences as well as similarities:

  - Whereas in 1959 the overwhelming proportion (almost 80%) of black children were growing up with two parents, today the majority are being raised in single-parent households.
  - Although the corresponding increase for young white children is far less steep, the actual numbers are much greater. By 1994, 3.9 million white children under age 6 were living with a single parent compared to 2.5 million blacks and 1.2 million Hispanics.

- The situation is more complicated, for there are several worlds of single parenthood.

FIGURE 4-6

MORE CHILDREN ARE BEING RAISED BY ONE UNMARRIED PARENT

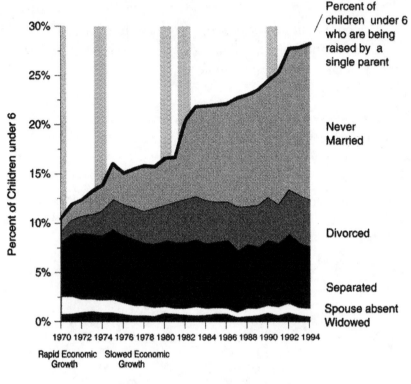

Cumulative percent by family type.

• The marked rise over the past quarter-century in the number of young children being brought up in single-parent families (now more than a quarter of all children under age 6) is due primarily to the growing number of unmarried parents.

• Information on the percentage of children in different forms of single-parent families has been available only since 1970, a period of slowed economic growth. An examination of the changes in rate over this period (including periods of economic recession indicated on the graph) reveals that unmarried single-parent families have been the most affected by short-term changes in the economy.

• The percentage of young children living with a divorced parent has also increased, but at a much slower rate.

FIGURE 4-7

SINGLE PARENTHOOD: A CHILD'S WORLD
OF FATHERS AS WELL AS MOTHERS

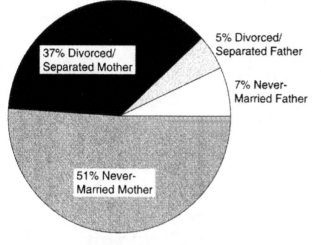

All children are under 6 years of age.

- As of 1994, over 10% of all children under age 6 in one-parent families were being raised by a single father. The majority of these fathers are unmarried rather than separated or divorced.

- Although the percentage of single-parent fathers is still relatively small, it has been growing steadily since the early 1960s and is likely to continue to grow, for reasons to be presented later in this chapter. This prospect takes on added significance because both the conditions and consequences of growing up with a single-parent father turn out to be somewhat different from being raised by a single-parent mother. (See Figures 4-10, 4-17, 4-18, 4-24, 4-26, and 4-28.)

- Whether the single parent is unmarried or divorced also makes a difference. Among the factors that account for these differential outcomes is that mothers and fathers who are either unmarried or divorced are themselves more likely to have grown up in family structures and broader social contexts similar to those in which they end up as adults.

- The next set of graphs addresses the nature of these contrasting circumstances and structures as a necessary prerequisite for understanding their developmental effects.

FIGURE 4–8

UNMARRIED MOTHERHOOD FOR WHOM?

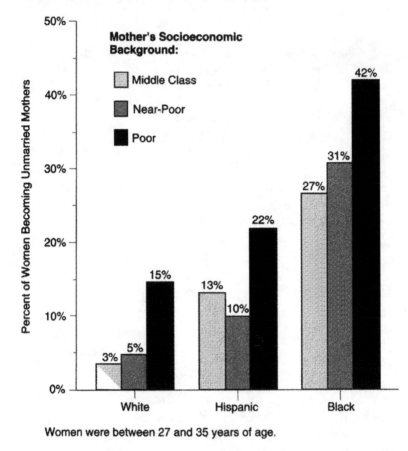

Women were between 27 and 35 years of age.

- The percentage of women bearing a child while unmarried varies markedly depending on the mother's socioeconomic and ethnic background:[3]

  - At each socioeconomic level, white women were the least likely to have a baby without being married, black women the most likely, with Hispanic women in between.
  - Similarly, but to a lesser extent, women from middle-class backgrounds were less likely to bear a child without being married compared to those who had grown up in near-poor or poor families.[4]

• The biggest difference is not the separate influences of socioeconomic and ethnic background but their combined, mutually reinforcing effects. This phenomenon is most clearly seen in the contrast between the percentage of unmarried mothers who had grown up in middle-class white families compared to their counterparts from poor black families. Such nonadditive, so-called synergistic effects are characteristic for processes of human development. Moreover, they operate in both directions: developmentally favorable conditions combine to accelerate processes of psychological growth, whereas impoverished or disruptive environments quicken the course of developmental disarray. But to accomplish their respective effects, both kinds of processes have to operate over extended periods of time.

FIGURE 4-9

UNMARRIED MOTHERHOOD ACROSS THE DECADES

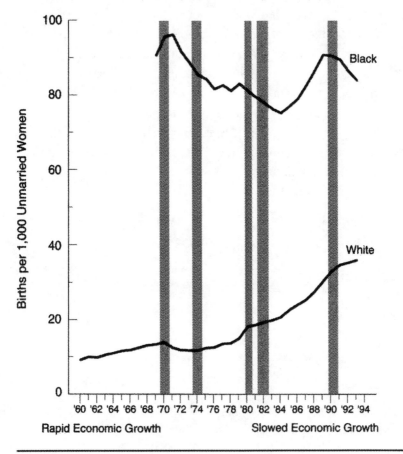

- The graph presents a paradox. As we already know, birth rates to un-married women are much higher for blacks than for whites. This has been true for the past two decades, despite marked fluctuations not clearly related to either long- or short-term changes in the economy.

- By contrast, birth rates to white unmarried women have been in-creasing steadily over the past three decades, especially during the period of slowed economic growth from the mid-1970s to the pres-ent. Moreover, white unmarried mothers appear to be the only one of the three major ethnic groups, married or unmarried, for whom birth rates are rising; all others have been falling steadily.[5]

• Once again we have evidence that other forces besides, and perhaps beyond, economics are driving the dramatic changes that have been occurring in American families over recent decades. As the next graph shows, some of these forces operate in the third dimension, producing both continuity and change from one generation to the next.

FIGURE 4–10

THE FAMILY A CHILD GROWS UP IN
SHAPES THE FAMILY THAT CHILD CREATES

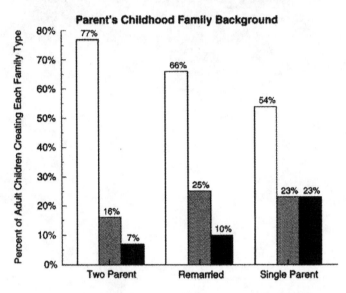

Parent's Childhood Family Background

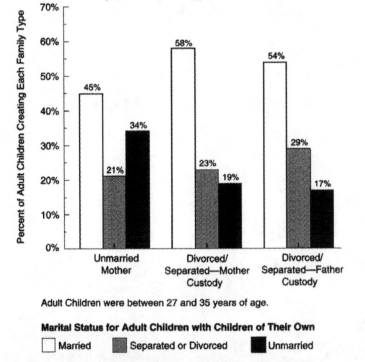

Forms of Single Parenthood Experienced in Childhood

Adult Children were between 27 and 35 years of age.

Marital Status for Adult Children with Children of Their Own

☐ Married   ▨ Separated or Divorced   ■ Unmarried

• Does the type of family structure in which a person is raised bear any relation to the family structure in which that person ends up as an adult with children of one's own? To investigate this question we took advantage of the cross-generational design of the NLSY sample.

• The great majority of children growing up in a two-parent family—married or remarried—ended up forming two-parent families of their own. By contrast, close to half (46%) of adults who had been raised by a single parent ended up as single parents themselves—half of them as unmarried and the remainder as separated or divorced.

• Marriage rates in the younger generation were somewhat lower for those who had been raised by remarried parents than for those of parents who remained together. This finding is consistent with a general pattern of somewhat greater developmental vulnerability for children and adolescents raised by remarried parents. However, this difference is far smaller than that for two-parent versus one-parent families.

• Did adults who had been brought up in a single-parent family exhibit differences in family formation depending on whether the single parent was unmarried or a divorced mother or a divorced father? The two main findings of this analysis focus on the contrasting marital patterns of grown children of divorce and of those who had been raised by an unmarried parent:
  • A majority of adult children brought up by a divorced parent ended up as married parents in adulthood.
  • Adults raised by an unmarried single parent showed a reverse pattern, with the majority becoming single parents—more (34%) unmarried than divorced, like their own mother had been.

FIGURE 4–11

WHO BECOMES AN UNMARRIED MOTHER? THE ROLE OF FAMILY STRUCTURE AND SOCIOECONOMIC BACKGROUND

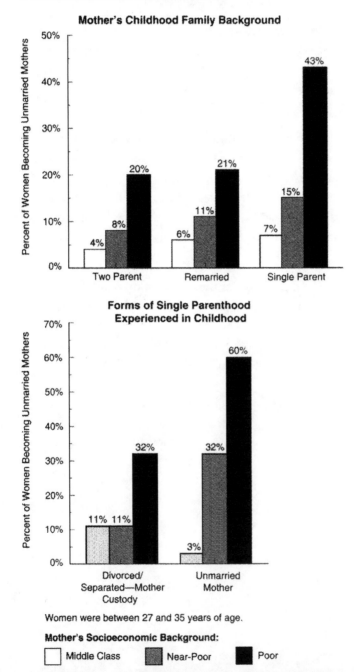

Women were between 27 and 35 years of age.

Mother's Socioeconomic Background:

☐ Middle Class   ▨ Near-Poor   ■ Poor

• The future mother's socioeconomic background—here measured primarily in terms of her parents' family income—is the strongest predictor of her later having a child without being married. But whether she herself grew up in a single-parent home also makes a big difference, particularly if her own mother was unmarried.

• Once again, the combined effects of social class and family structure are greater than the separate influence of each, with 43% of women growing up in a poor, one-parent family themselves ending up having a child while unmarried.

• Only 7% of daughters from single-parent, middle-class families become single-parent mothers themselves. In this regard, bear in mind that the reported results are based on interviews primarily with the mothers themselves. Hence the possibility arises that women from middle-class backgrounds may be less ready to acknowledge an out-of-wedlock birth than their counterparts who had grown up in poverty, where such births are much more common.

• Overall, the principal determinant of whether a woman becomes a single parent, particularly one who is unmarried, appears to be the income level of the family in which she was raised. As documented in the two graphs that follow, that income is lowest for unmarried mothers in general and for single black mothers in particular.

FIGURE 4–12

INCOME IS LINKED TO FAMILY STRUCTURE FOR FAMILIES WITH YOUNG CHILDREN

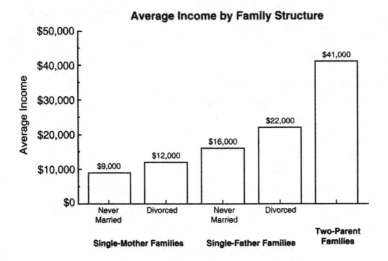

Average Income by Family Structure

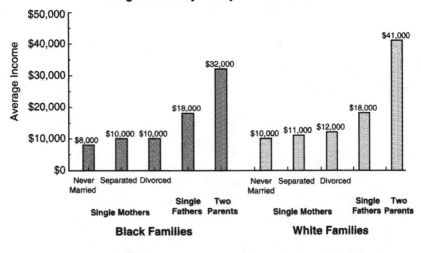

Average Income by Family Structure and Race

- The biggest contrast in income is between that for two-parent families and for single-parent families in all their forms. Moreover, that contrast is even greater for white families than for black—a range of $31,000 for the former compared with $24,000 for the latter.[6] (As documented in the next chapter, a similar contrast appears at the international level: in terms of family income, rich and poor families are further apart in the United States than in any other developed nation.)

• Even more critical for the well-being and development of children is the variation in income across different forms of single parenthood, with never-married single-parent black mothers having the lowest income of all: $8,000 per year.

• The array of dollar figures presented in this figure leads directly to another major social change that has been taking place in American family life: level of income for families with young children is increasingly being determined by the extent to which their mothers are working, especially mothers in single-parent families.

FIGURE 4-13

WORKING MOTHERS ACROSS THE DECADES

Young Children with Mothers in the Workforce, by Family Structure

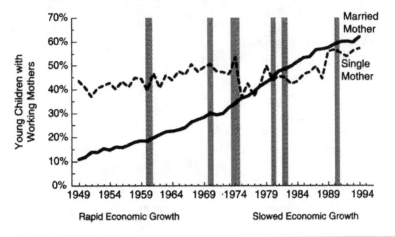

- Ever since 1949, when the Bureau of Labor Statistics first began to gather and report the information, the results have shown a marked rise in the percentage of working mothers in two-parent families with young children. From the perspective of long-term social change, the increase has been dramatic—from close to 10% in 1949 to just over 60% today.

- This trend has persisted essentially at the same rate through the successive periods of rapid and slowed economic growth, with only minimal response to short-term periods of economic recession and recovery. Clearly this major social change has been driven mainly by other than purely economic forces.

- In sharp contrast, the percentage of single mothers in the workforce was much higher to start with and has increased only modestly over time—from close to 45% in 1949 to 52% by 1994.[7]

- Throughout this whole period, the rate of participation in the labor force by single mothers has fluctuated appreciably in response to short-term economic recessions and recoveries.

- In short, many single women with young children have to work to make ends meet, but the uncertainty of their jobs forces them to drop in and out of the labor market.

FIGURE 4–14

WORKING PARENTS WITH YOUNG CHILDREN

Labor Force Participation Rates:

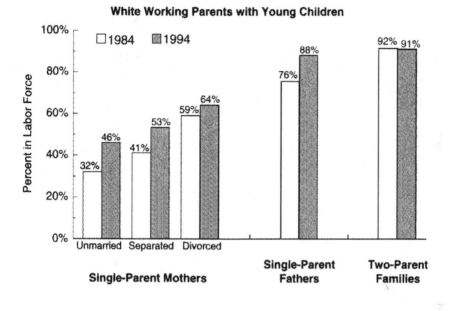

White Working Parents with Young Children

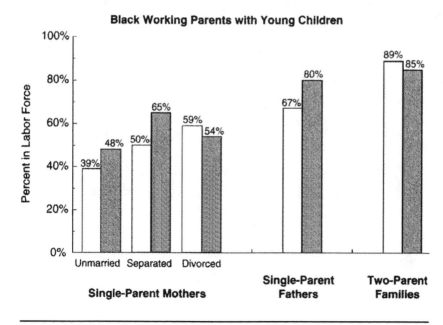

Black Working Parents with Young Children

• This figure tells two stories, black and white, running parallel through time but still differing in important respects.

• Over the past decade, an increasing percentage of single parents of young children—fathers as well as mothers—have been entering the workforce. Although in percentage terms the increases may not seem large, the actual number of new workers is substantial. Since 1984, about 1.3 million more single parents with children under age 6 have entered the labor force (with about a quarter of the increase attributable to the growth in the number of single-parent fathers).

• The increased labor force participation of single-parent fathers invites a number of possible hypotheses, but we have not been able to find any systematic evidence bearing on the issue. With respect to single-parent mothers, however, the findings point to a plausible explanation based on the differing patterns for blacks and whites:

  • Although profiles of participation are similar for the two groups, the rates for unmarried and separated black mothers are higher than those for whites.
  • Incomes of single-parent mothers, particularly those in black families, are the lowest of the low—well below the official poverty line. Over the past decade government cash supports and other benefits to poor families have been reduced substantially, to the point that single-parent mothers are not able to provide for the basic needs of their children, especially the very young. Hence they enter the labor force.

• Mothers with young children confront yet another problem. It is one thing to be willing and wanting to work; it is another to find a job and hold it.

FIGURE 4–15

WORKING PARENTS WHO CANNOT GET A JOB

Unemployment Rates for Families with Children Under Age 6

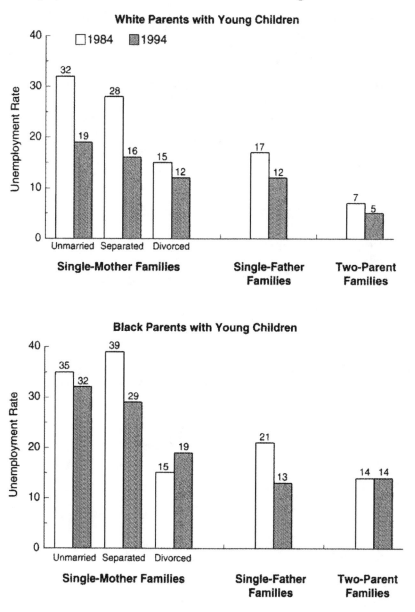

- Visually the paired graphs present a left-right reversal of their dual predecessors. Translating form into substance reveals a poignant paradox: those who need and want a job most have the highest unemployment rates, and the burden of providing for their young children falls most heavily on single-parent mothers, particularly those who are both black and unmarried.

- To be sure, over the past decade, unemployment rates have been falling, but again more so for whites than for blacks. But we know that proportionally more black than white unmarried and separated mothers entered the labor force over this period—needing work, seeking work, but not finding it.

- A similarly contrasting pattern appears for white and black single-parent fathers but with much lower unemployment rates.

- Unemployment rates for divorced mothers are appreciably better, perhaps because many are able to get along with child-support payments from their ex-husbands, but even here black mothers have lost ground. Whereas since 1984 unemployment rates have fallen for their white counterparts, theirs have risen.

- One other part of the story is not shown in the figure. The majority of single-parent mothers who do work—both black and white—are working full time. But here, too, despite the higher unemployment rate, the proportion of black mothers working full time is higher—in this instance, much higher—than for whites. In 1994, the percentage for all black single mothers was 76%, compared to 29% for whites. So much for the claim that most black single-parent mothers are content to stay on welfare.

- A full-time job, especially for a one-parent family, increasingly presents yet another problem: Who will take care of the children, especially when they are still quite young?

FIGURE 4–16

NEED FOR AND ANNUAL COST OF CHILD CARE

Families with Employed Mothers:

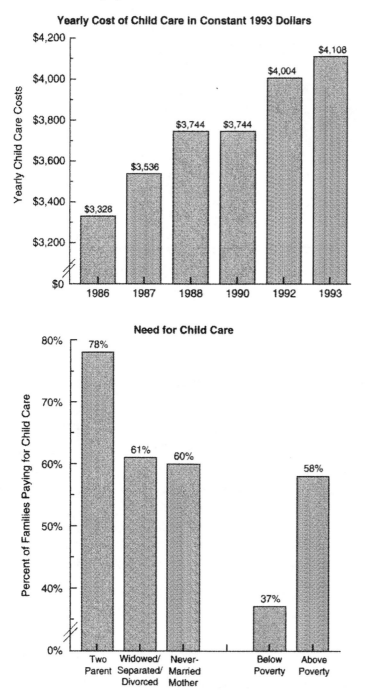

Yearly Cost of Child Care in Constant 1993 Dollars

Need for Child Care

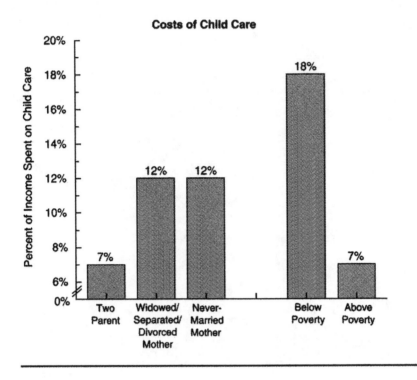

Costs of Child Care

• As documented in a recent special study conducted by the U.S. Census, the cost of child care has been rising, and the burden is falling most heavily on those who can afford it least yet need it most: single-parent mothers and families living below the poverty line.[8]

• The extent of the need, and the stresses that it creates, are reflected in the fact that families who can afford it least spend the largest proportion of their meager incomes to obtain child care: 18% by families living in poverty and 12% by single-parent mothers, compared to 7% for two-parent families and those whose incomes are above the poverty line.

• We turn next to yet another form of parenthood. It focuses primarily on the mother's age, which turns out to have consequences not only for her child's future but also her own.

FIGURE 4–17

SEXUAL ACTIVITY AND TEENAGERS

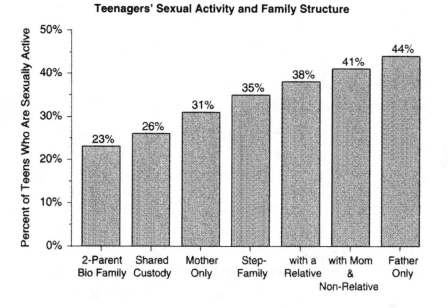

Teenagers' Sexual Activity and Family Structure

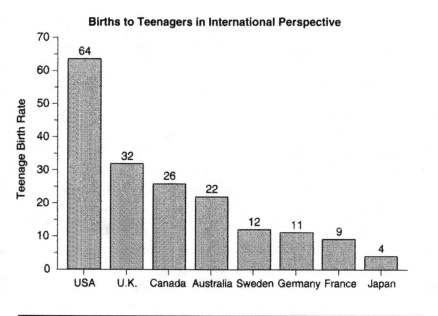

Births to Teenagers in International Perspective

- In many segments of American society, sexual activity earlier and earlier in adolescence is increasingly becoming the norm.[9] From a developmental perspective, what is most significant about this growing behavior pattern is its occurrence during the period of transition into young adulthood and its attendant expectations of greater independence and self-direction, for which the young person has been prepared through prior experience in the family, the school, and other societal settings serving this purpose.

- For a young female, sexual activity entails the possibility of bearing and having to care for a child of her own. It is one thing for a teenager to go through this challenging experience while married, surrounded by experienced parents and family members who respond unasked with practical help and warm emotional support; it is quite another for an unmarried girl with no easy claim on the child's father, for either emotional support or practical help, let alone financial assistance. It means having to grow up too soon at an age and under circumstances that, in the long run, jeopardize the development of competence and character.

- Most important in this graph are not the differences between particular percentages but the general direction in which they steadily rise, moving from the two-parent biological through a single mother, and a remarried family, to relatives, nonrelatives, and ending back with a primary family tie—the father.

- Why should such a biologically driven behavior as sexual activity vary systematically depending on the family structure in which the young person has been living? A key to a possible answer is found in the fact that we have seen the same pattern before in relation to other types of behavior: the growing cynicism in the beliefs and behaviors of youth, rising youth delinquency, family disruption, and the consistency with which the United States stands in first place in international comparisons of indexes of family disorganization. Even when only the white population is considered, the United States is still in first place in teenage childbearing, with a rate twice as high as England's, its nearest competitor.

• In calling attention to these convergent relationships, there is no intent to equate sexual activity with antisocial or immoral attitudes and behaviors. Indeed, it may be argued that sexual activity, if engaged in responsibly, is today a part of typical adolescent development in our culture. But if so, why should it be related to different forms of family structure? Critical to the answer is yet another question: which youth are most likely to engage in unprotected sex? The evidence on this score indicates that risky behaviors, including unprotected sex, occur more frequently among families in which there is a single parent or in which family disruption has occurred.

FIGURE 4–18

THE RISKS OF TEENAGE CHILDBEARING
EXTEND ACROSS GENERATIONS

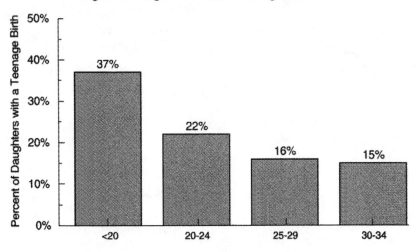

Age of Teenager's Mother at Teenager's Birth

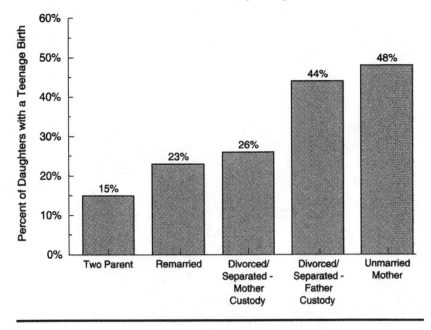

Woman's Childhood Family Background

• A child whose mother had a baby when she was a teenager is more likely to become a teenaged mother herself than one whose mother had her child in later life. That is not the only way in which risk can extend across generations.

• The family environment in which a teenager grows up can influence her own life course development. Children who grow up in a two-parent family have a much smaller chance of becoming young mothers than those who grow up in other family forms; the probability is highest for those raised by an unmarried mother.

• Although the risk is generally greater for children raised in single-parent families, it is also higher in married families in which one spouse is a stepparent. Finally, children living with a divorced father may be at special risk.[10]

• All of these findings are consistent with the data on sexual activity. As we shall see later in this chapter, risk in other developmental domains is also reduced for children from two-parent families. In short, growing up with two parents can be a protective factor for the rest of one's life.

• But again, that is not the whole story. Money also matters.

FIGURE 4–19

UNMARRIED TEENAGE CHILDBEARING
AND FAMILY STRUCTURE

The Role of Family Income

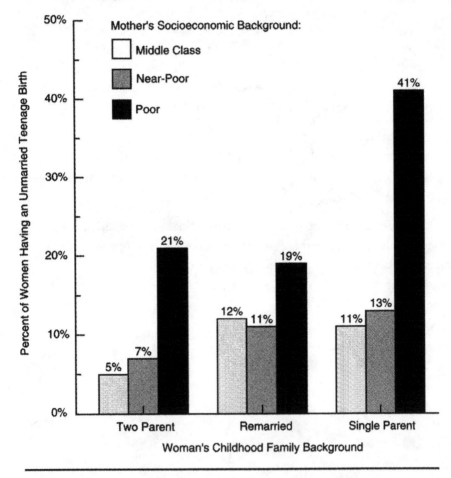

- Family income can make a big difference for the effects of family structure on the life course of female adolescents. Although daughters of single parents are at greater risk of becoming unwed mothers, growing up below the poverty level raises that risk substantially.

- The rate of early unwed childbearing is greatly reduced for the near-poor and middle class. This is especially true for daughters who grew up in a single-parent family. Those from single-parent homes above the poverty line resemble two-parent families in which one parent is remarried. Indeed, daughters from single-parent families above poverty are only slightly more at risk than those with two parents.[11]

• The main message of this figure is perhaps by now all too familiar: the developmentally disruptive effects of poverty on families and children are even stronger than those of single parenthood. But the thrust of that message is virtually reversed by equally compelling evidence, to be presented in the next chapter, that the principal producer of family poverty in contemporary American society is the escalating growth of single-parent families. The graphs that follow prepare the ground for resolving this seeming contradiction.

FIGURE 4–20
BIRTH RATES IN FOUR WORLDS

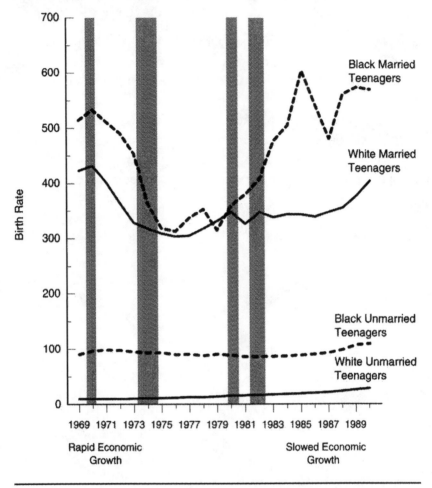

- This graph discloses some striking contrasts in the pathways through time of four major groups of teenaged mothers in American society.[12]

- The first feature that captures attention is the turnaround in teenaged childbearing among young married black girls, who also have the highest birth rate of all the groups. A sharp decline during the period of rapid economic growth still taking place during the early 1970s soon gives way to an equally steep rise in the slowed and fluctuating economy of the 1980s. As we have come to expect,

white married teenagers follow a similar course but at a more sub-
dued level and pace. The higher birth rate for married teenagers (in
comparison to their unmarried peers) reflects the greater propensity
of married teenagers to have children.

• By contrast, both black and white unmarried teenagers exhibit an
even course, with rates rising only slightly over the entire period.
The only similarity with the trend for the married is the higher fertility of young black women, which again remains essentially stable
over the three decades, with minimal reaction to short-term fluctuations in the economy.

• Given these findings, why is there a renewed concern about
teenaged childbearing? The trends presented here indicate that
birth rates for black and white teenaged girls, married and unmarried, are at about the same levels today as they were in 1970. However, the data as presented obscure some of the most dramatic
changes that have occurred in teenaged childbearing over the past
three decades. This is so because birth rates are calculated on a
within-group basis and do not reflect the changing size of the four
groups being compared in this graph.

• What has really been happening to teenaged childbearing over this
thirty year period? The next graph gives the answer.

FIGURE 4-21

TEENAGE CHILDBEARING: MARRIED VS. UNMARRIED

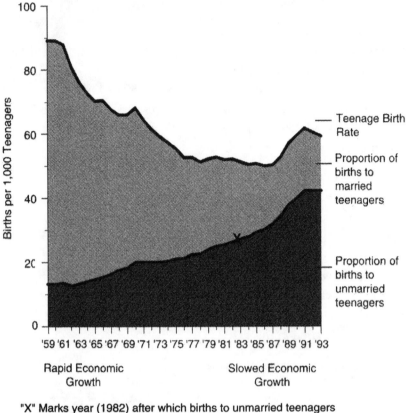

Rapid Economic Growth

Slowed Economic Growth

"X" Marks year (1982) after which births to unmarried teenagers exceeded those to married teenagers.

This is a cumulative graph.

- The curve at the top of the graph looks like the one in the previous figure depicting changes across the years in the birth rate for black married teenaged girls. Like its predecessor, this curve too shows a steady and marked decline through most of the 1970s, followed by a rise in the 1980s. This curve, however, does not apply just to blacks. It depicts changes over time in the birth rate for all teenaged girls in the United States—white, black, and every other ethnic group. But how come it most resembles the graph for just black teenagers? And what produced the turnaround for all?

• The answers to these questions turn out to be somewhat complex. The two areas below the upper curve are in fact where the answers lie. The area directly below the bottom curve documents the rise in births to all unmarried teenagers of whatever background, whereas the upper band reflects a complementary but much more marked decline in births to all married teenage girls.

• Between the two bands, X marks the year (1982) after which the majority of births to teenaged mothers in the United States shifted from the married to the unmarried. Since that time, births to married teenage girls have been declining, while those for the unmarried have been steadily rising. It is this switchover that accounts for the turnaround in the overall teenaged birth rate in the early 1980s.

• What about blacks and whites? Did each of these groups also experience a reversal in the percentage of births to teenaged girls?

FIGURE 4–22

TEENAGED CHILDBEARING:
A TURNAROUND FOR BLACKS AND WHITES?

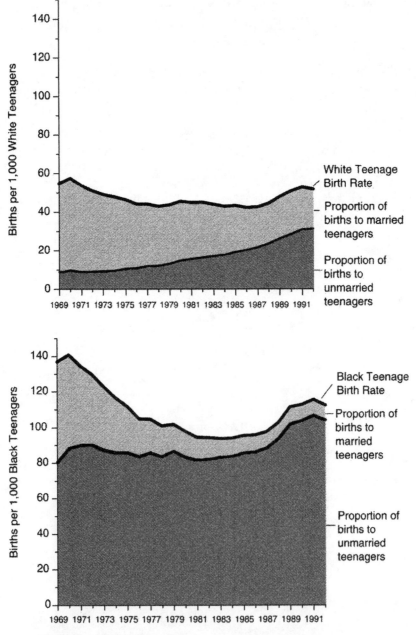

These are cumulative graphs.

- Birth rates for black teenaged girls have indeed shown a reversal, going down in the 1970s but then rising again in the 1980s, mostly because of the sharp decline in births to young married mothers during the earlier decade, accompanied by a more moderate increase in births to the unmarried in the 1980s.

- The picture for white teenaged girls is rather different. The turn-around—if one can call it that—is barely perceptible, mainly because the falling births to the married tend to be balanced off by the rising births to the unmarried.

- For both groups, the proportion of births to unmarried teenaged mothers is rising markedly. To be sure, this statement is qualified given that the rise in births to teenaged girls is a reflection of the broader phenomenon of increasing births to unmarried women in general, and that birth rates for those between ages 20 and 30 are much higher than those for teenaged girls.

- This qualification is outweighed by a more consequential reality: having a baby as an unmarried teenager can affect the future development not only of the child but also of the mother herself.

- Now we call attention to a developmental domain for which the developmental risk associated with growing up in a single-parent family is greater for males than for females: dropping out—not only out of high school, but college as well.

The graph that follows sets the stage by presenting how education is linked to family structure in the parents' generation.

FIGURE 4-23

EDUCATION ATTAINED AND CURRENT FAMILY SITUATION OF PARENTS OF YOUNG CHILDREN

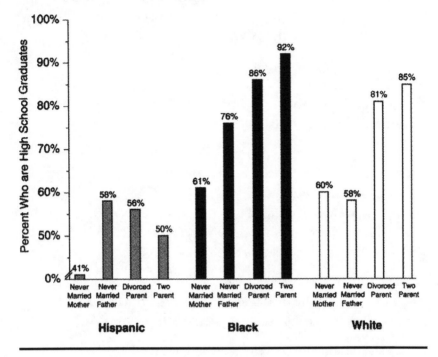

- Among parents who form two-parent families, the percentage graduating from high school is higher for blacks than for whites. To a lesser degree, the same is true of divorced parents and unmarried fathers.

- Hispanics include a greater proportion of whites than of blacks. Hence, their inclusion decreases the high school graduation rate of white parents more than black parents. The lower graduation rates of Hispanic parents may reflect problems with English as a second language.

- Other differences in family structure fall into an expected pattern. As in income, never-married mothers have the least education.

FIGURE 4–24

DOES FAMILY STRUCTURE MAKE A DIFFERENCE?

Dropping Out of High School or College

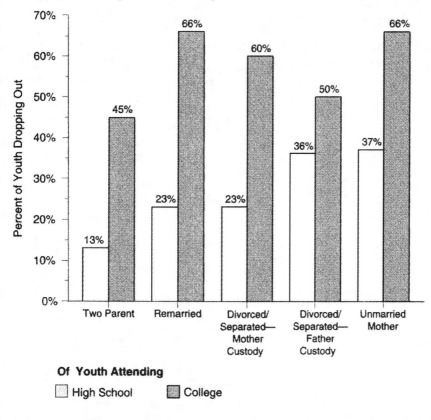

Of Youth Attending
☐ High School   ▨ College

- In general, young people who drop out of high school or college are more likely to have grown up in a single-parent family.

- There are also some interesting—and even surprising—exceptions from what one might have expected.

  - Long-term effects are even more powerful than the short term. Thus, rates for dropping out of college are even higher than those for high school.

  - This difference is particularly marked with respect to remarried parents compared to married parents who have stayed together. Up until now, developmental risks associated with growing up with stepparents have been only slightly higher than those for youth growing up with two biological parents. Similarly, for those dropping out of college, the risks were lower for children of divorce with the father having custody.

• Could parents' higher education and income be factors here? The next two graphs speak to this issue.

FIGURE 4–25

WHAT MATTERS MORE: FAMILY STRUCTURE OR INCOME?

Dropping Out of High School

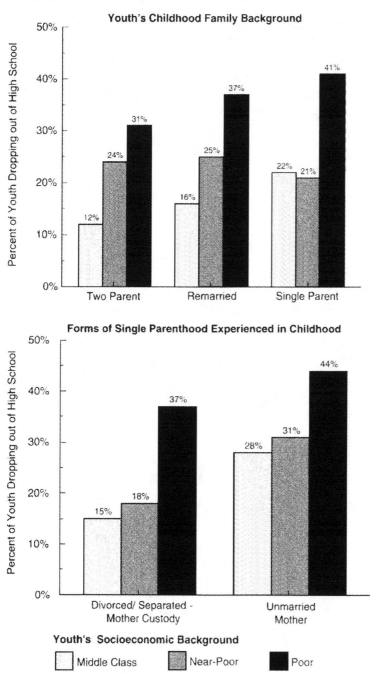

- Once again, family structure matters, but family income—in particular, living in poverty—matters even more.

- Especially for families in poverty, family structure comes back into the picture. It is children of poor, unmarried single mothers who most often drop out of high school.

- Similarly, for those growing up in two-parent families, the greater developmental vulnerability of youth raised in remarried families is most pronounced for the poor.

FIGURE 4–26

PARENTS' EDUCATION MAKES A BIG DIFFERENCE

Family Structure and Dropping Out of High School

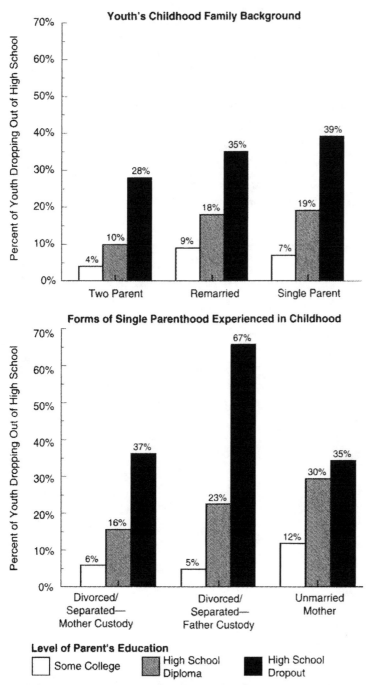

- The figure looks much like its predecessor, except that now it is parents' education that wields the greater power, and its effect is to reduce substantially the risk of dropping out associated with growing up in a single-parent family. For youth who had at least one parent with exposure to a college education, the high school dropout rate never rises above 12%. It is a negligible 4% for children raised in a two-parent family.

- At the opposite pole are youth from one-parent families in which one or the other parent had been a high school dropout. Here the probability of like following like was especially high for children of divorce living in their father's custody. For this group, the dropout rate was exceptionally high—67%—compared to 37% for those living in the custody of their divorced mother.

FIGURE 4–27

WHICH IS MORE POWERFUL:
SOCIAL CLASS OR PARENTS' EDUCATION?

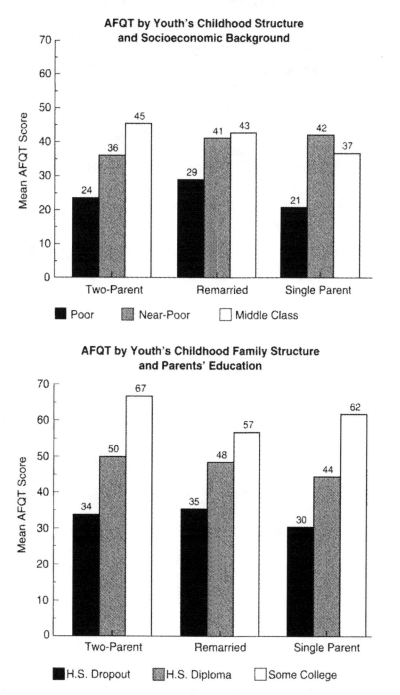

AFQT by Youth's Childhood Structure and Socioeconomic Background

■ Poor   ▨ Near-Poor   ☐ Middle Class

AFQT by Youth's Childhood Family Structure and Parents' Education

■ H.S. Dropout   ▨ H.S. Diploma   ☐ Some College

• The Armed Forces Qualification Test (AFQT), which had been administered to youth in the NLSY sample, provides a direct test of the relative predictive power of family structure versus parents' education, with rather clear-cut results.

• Without exception, the level of their parents' education showed a stronger relationship to the youth's AFQT score than the structure of the family in which they had been raised. Moreover, the effects of education were just as powerful for youth raised in single-parent families as for those in two-parent homes. However, as the last two figures in this chapter demonstrate, the developmentally disruptive power of poverty is far more wide ranging across both space and time.

FIGURE 4–28

WHO ENDS UP IN POVERTY AS A YOUNG ADULT?

Childhood Family Structure and Parents' Education

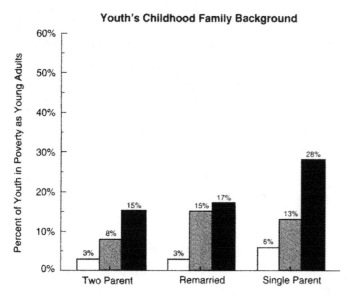

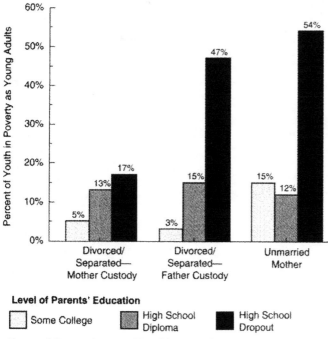

Level of Parents' Education

☐ Some College   ▨ High School   ■ High School
                          Diploma   Dropout

Young adults were between 27 and 35 years of age.

- The pattern of results is all too familiar, but the message is one of hope. Raising parents' level of education—particularly enabling them to finish high school—can significantly reduce the risk that their children will end up in poverty as young adults.

- Completing high school is especially important for unmarried mothers and single-parent fathers. For those who drop out of high school, about half of their children will live in poverty as adults.

FIGURE 4–29

WHO ENDS UP IN POVERTY AS A YOUNG ADULT?

Childhood Family Structure and Income

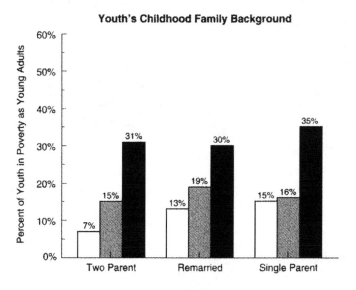

Youth's Childhood Family Background

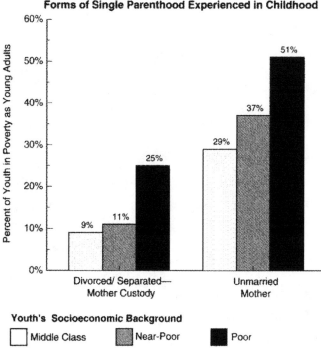

Forms of Single Parenthood Experienced in Childhood

Youth's Socioeconomic Background

☐ Middle Class   ▨ Near-Poor   ■ Poor

Young adults were between 27 and 35 years of age.

- Low family income remains a strong enemy, especially for young adults who grew up with an unmarried mother.

- As revealed in many of the cross-generational graphs presented in this chapter, it is the combination of structure and socioeconomic level of the family in which one is raised that wields the greatest power in influencing the competence and character of their grown-up children. Those who grow up in poor, single-parent families are at greatest risk, particularly when the mother is unmarried; those raised in two-parent middle-class families appear to remain relatively unscathed.

LOOKING TO THE FUTURE

The authors of this book agreed that each chapter would end with a projection of future trends, an evaluation of their probability, and an assessment of their implications for the competence and character of the next generation. However, in the light of the findings documented in this chapter, such a projection seems premature. The reason is that one of the most compelling conclusions these findings confirm is the emergence in the United States of a new and separate social class, with a formal identity validated in law, multicultural in composition (an *e pluribus unum* no longer existing in the rest of our society), and, in the absence of radical changes in policy and action on a national scale, destined to increase in numbers and to share a common and tragic fate for this generation and the next. That class lives in a national ghetto with ever-expanding borders meticulously defined by the poverty line.

This growing phenomenon, already encompassing one-quarter of all young children in the United States, has profound implications not only for the future of the nation's poor families but for the society as a whole: its economy, productivity, and the well-being and character of its people.

Accordingly, we defer any projections for the future pending a systematic analysis, in the chapter that follows, of the nature and evolution of this new world of American families and its implications for the development of the children and youth who grow up within its borders.

APPENDIX: ANALYSES CONDUCTED USING THE NATIONAL LONGITUDINAL SURVEY OF YOUTH

In order to investigate the effects of the family context on the developing child, we used the National Longitudinal Survey of Youth, a study of over 12,000 youths ages 14–22 years, first interviewed in 1979 and reinterviewed every year since. This data set allowed for the investigation of the enduring effects of childhood family structure into the young adult years. The sample is overrepresentative of low-income and minority families, so that inferences may be drawn about these subpopulations. The data, however, can be weighted to estimate these effects in a nationally representative sample of youths born between 1957 and 1965.

Individual case weights are assigned using three types of adjustments: (1) the reciprocal of the probability of selection at the baseline interview (which accounts for the oversampling of ethnic minority and low-income youths), (2) adjustment for differential response rates in the screening, baseline, and follow-up interviews, and (3) adjustment for some random variation and sample undercoverage. For all of the analyses performed in this chapter and the next, the cases were weighted using the weight assigned to the case during the year in which the dependent variable is assessed.

Although useful in making inferences about the nature of the association between childhood conditions and adult outcomes, this study cannot inform us about the effects of growing up today in these same contexts. Single parenthood today is not the same as single parenthood in the 1960s, when the youths in this sample were growing up. Furthermore, the forces influencing individual development do not work independently but mutually reinforce each other. The analyses we have performed cannot account for these processes. Despite the cautions, however, the analyses do provide some understanding of the association between childhood experiences and adult outcomes for children growing up in this country.

Variables Created from the NLSY

Childhood Family Structure. We created the categories using family information data gathered during the 1988 interview:

Two-parent families: Those in which the youth was born and grew up with two biological parents, at least until his or her fifteenth year.

Unmarried-mother families: Those in which the youth was born to a single unmarried mother and lived with only that parent for at least the first five years of his or her life.

Divorced/separated—mother custody families: Those in which the youth was born to two biological parents, but at age 15 is living only with his or her biological mother and no stepparent ever lived with him or her.

Divorced/separated—father custody families: Those in which the youth was born to two biological parents but at age 15 is living only with his or her biological father and no stepparent ever lived with him or her.

Remarried families: Those in which the youth was born to two biological parents but at age 15 is living with one biological parent and one stepparent.

Family Socioeconomic Status: Family income data for 1978 were analyzed for youths who were under age 18 and living at home in 1979:

Poor families: Those defined as "in poverty" using information on the family's poverty status in 1978 collected in 1979.

Near-poor families: Those defined as in the lowest or second quintile (but not below the poverty line) using 1978 income cutoffs for families published in the *Statistical Abstract of the United States.*

Middle-income families: Those defined as in the third quintile using 1978 income cutoffs for families published in the *Statistical Abstract.*

Parents' Educational Level. This was created using information on the mothers' and fathers' highest grade completed collected in 1979. The parent whose education was analyzed depended on the family structure of the youth's childhood. Specifically, for two-parent families, the higher of the mother or father's educational level was used; for unmarried mother and divorced/separated—mother custody families, the mother's educational level was used; for divorced/separated—father custody families, the father's educational level was used; for remarried families, the educational level of the biological parent with which the youth lived was used.

High School Dropout. Youths who had completed less than twelfth grade by the age of 20 years are classified as high school dropouts.

College Dropout. Youths who entered college by the 1991 interview but had not completed four years of school are classified as college dropouts.

Youths' Young Adult Family Structure. Youths who had a biological child by the 1992 interview are classified by their 1992 marital status as never married, divorced/separated, or married.

AFQT score. Youths' AFQT score, collected during the 1980 interview, but recalculated in 1989, was used.

Youths' Young Adult Poverty Status. Family poverty status in 1992 was used to assess the youth's poverty status in young adulthood.

5

POVERTY AND THE
NEXT GENERATION

This chapter is directed mainly to the future. The term "Next Generation" refers to the children of today, who will be the adults of tomorrow. The poverty in which these children are growing up already exists, and we have the relevant statistics to analyze. Obviously we do not have data for the adults of tomorrow, so we must rely heavily on projection from present findings. The strategy we employ is not only statistical but developmental. In accord with our ecological model, we begin by looking at the development of poverty itself from the perspective of space and time. To be sure, the poor are always with us, so we cannot afford to start too far back.

We begin with the time, now a quarter of a century ago, when poverty in the United States was first given an official definition for government use. That definition has been dutifully repeated in each annual report of the U.S. Census on *Poverty in the United States*. Both its key provisions and their origin are relevant to our purpose. Fortunately, both of these elements are included in the official definition:

This definition was established as the official definition of poverty for statistical use in all Executive departments by the Bureau of the Budget (in Circular No. A-46). [It was] based on a definition developed by

146

the Social Security Administration in 1964 and revised in 1969 and 1981 by interagency committees. . . .

The original poverty index provided a range of income cutoffs adjusted by such factors as family size, sex of the family head, and the number of children under 18 years old. . . . At the core of this definition of poverty was the economy food plan, the least costly of four nutritionally adequate food plans developed by the Department of Agriculture. It was determined from [the department's] survey of food consumption that families of three or more persons spent approximately one-third of their income on food; the poverty level was therefore set at three times the cost of the economy food plan. For smaller families and persons living alone, the cost of the economy food plan was multiplied by factors that were slightly higher in order to compensate for the relatively larger fixed expenses of these smaller households.[1]

As a result of recommendations made by the Federal Interagency Committee in 1969, the decision was made that annual adjustments in poverty thresholds henceforth "be based on changes in the Consumer Price Index rather than on changes in the cost of food included in the economy food plan."[2] Once the thresholds were established, they were applied by the Bureau of the Census to demographic data from previous years to calculate changes in poverty rates and related family information going as far back as 1959. It is these data that we use to trace the changing nature of American poverty for families with young children from that year up to the present.

In the first part of the chapter, we present the results of this analysis. We then turn to our projections about poverty and the next generation of Americans—the children in poverty today who will be adults in the next century.

We begin by looking at today's poverty from an international perspective. As the basis for comparison in this analysis, the original authors essentially used the American definition of poverty.[3]

FIGURE 5-1

CHILDREN IN POVERTY

Developed Nations

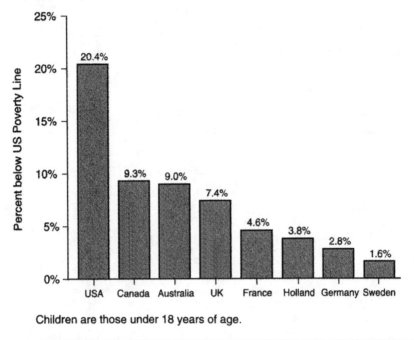

Children are those under 18 years of age.

- Among developed countries, the United States has the highest percentage of children living in poverty.[4]

- Next come other English-speaking countries, with West European nations trailing well behind.

FIGURE 5–2

RICH AND POOR FAMILIES ARE FURTHEST APART
IN THE UNITED STATES

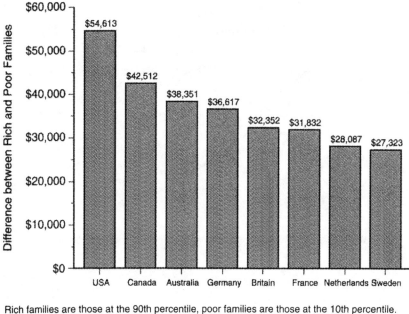

Rich families are those at the 90th percentile, poor families are those at the 10th percentile.
Values are difference in after-tax income of a family of four.
Children are those under 18 years of age.

- The title of the figure states the major finding.

- In the United States, yearly incomes for families with children ranged from an average of $10,923 for low-income parents to $65,536, for high-income parents, compared to a country with one of the smallest ranges, Sweden, where incomes varied from $18,129 to $46,152.

- A comparison of this graph with the preceding one reveals that, in general among economically developed nations, it is the more well-to-do countries in which incomes for families with children vary the most, although there are some exceptions. For example, in Germany incomes for families with children cover a considerable range, but not very many of the children are living in poverty.

• In a recent report, the authors make a further statement about the significance of their findings:

> While the United States has a higher level of income than most of our countries, it is the high- and middle-income children who reap the benefits (and much more the former than the latter). Low-income American children suffer in both absolute and relative terms. The average low-income child in 17 other countries is at least one-third better off than is the average low-income American child.[5]

FIGURE 5–3

CHILDREN IN POVERTY AND THE STATE OF THE ECONOMY

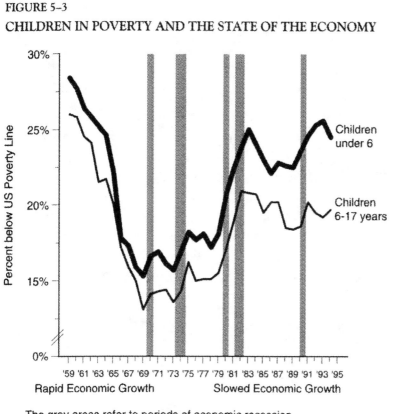

The gray areas refer to periods of economic recession.

- During the period of rapid economic growth, the percentage of children growing up in poverty declined sharply.

- During the subsequent period of slowed economic growth, poverty rates rose markedly, especially for families with younger children, thus widening the gap between the two age groups.[6]

- During short-term recessions, poverty rates for both age groups increased, particularly during the period of reduced economic growth starting in the mid-1970s. However, these fluctuations in rate are consistently smaller than, and are overridden by, the broader changes associated with the general decline in the level of the nation's economic growth that took hold in the late 1970s and has continued into the 1990s.

- Nevertheless, the impact of short-term recessions on the lives of poor families should not be underestimated, for they often involve loss of a job for the family breadwinner, which, beyond its economic effects, can lead to disruption of family relationships and processes influencing the subsequent course of development for children and youth.

- In general, the poverty rate for younger children was more affected by both short- and long-term changes in the state of the economy than was the rate for school-aged children. In particular, the risk of poverty, both short term and long term, has been especially high for young children and their families during the recent period of decline in the nation's economic growth. As a result, the gap in poverty rates between younger versus older children has widened in the last few years, with the former now standing at one-quarter of all children under 6, compared to 19% for the age group between 6 and 18.

- The overriding fact is that in a period of declining economic growth, poverty rates are rising for both age groups. Yet there is a striking exception to this general trend.

FIGURE 5–4

YOUNG AND OLD IN POVERTY

Percentage of Children under 6 and Adults 65 and over in Poverty

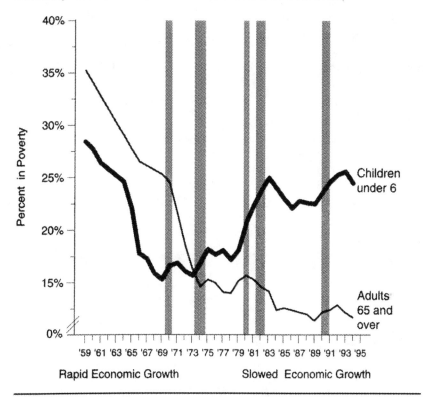

- When the economy was prospering, both young and old moved out of poverty at a rapid rate.

- When economic growth declined, the percentage of young children in poverty rose, but the elderly, who had social security benefits, held their ground.

- A comparison of this graph with the preceding ones reveals that short-term periods of recession and recovery affected the poverty rate for the elderly even less than for older children.

- Even during a period of slowed economic growth, social policies providing income support (like social security) can make a big difference.

• The graph raises some related questions: What is the risk of poverty for other age groups? Are youth beyond age 18 not as likely to be poor? As the elderly get older, do they continue to be as well protected against dying in poverty? And which age group is least likely to live in poverty?

• The next graph provides a beginning answer to these questions.

FIGURE 5–5

WHO ARE THE POOREST AMERICANS TODAY?

Poverty by Age Group

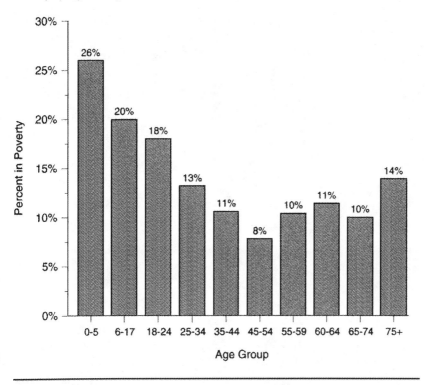

- In today's economy, from age 45 downward, the younger one is, the greater is the risk of ending up poor.

- This was not true three decades ago. Then, the old were much poorer than the young. By the mid-1970s, however, the poverty rate for both children and young adults aged 18–24 began to match that for 55 to 60 year olds.

- What does all this have to do with poverty and the next generation? The answer rests on the fact that younger children tend to have younger parents. Of all adults, this is the age group at highest risk for living in poverty.

- Far more influential than a parent's age are several other factors. Perhaps the most persistent of these is the family's ethnic background.

FIGURE 5–6

YOUNG CHILDREN IN POVERTY

Three Ethnic Groups

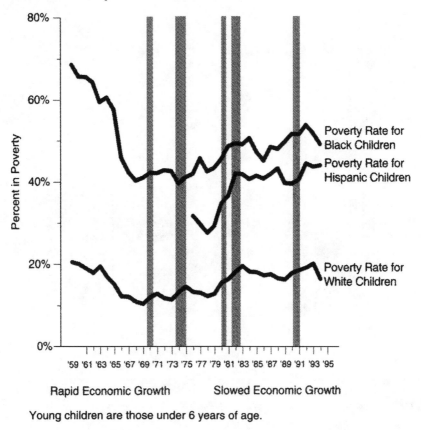

Young children are those under 6 years of age.

• There was a sharp decline in the percentage of young black children growing up in poverty during the period of rapid economic growth in the 1960s and early 1970s. To be sure, the percentage of decrease was about the same for blacks and whites (49% for the former, 48% for the latter). However, this fact overlooks a profound change in the social realities experienced by most black families with young children. Whereas in 1959 only a minority (31%) of black children under age 6 were not growing up in poverty, by 1967 that minority had become a substantial majority (61%).

- In the subsequent period of slowed economic growth (when data on Hispanic families first become available), the poverty rate in all three ethnic groups rose appreciably, but the sharp drop in poverty level observed for black families in the earlier period of general prosperity was not matched by an equally rapid return into poverty, so the racial gap did not increase substantially. In this respect, black families appear to be holding their own. Nevertheless, throughout both periods, minority families have been more affected by short- and long-term changes in the economy than have their white counterparts.

- A second striking trend is the rising poverty rate for young Hispanic children during the period of slowed economic growth.[8]

- How is one to explain these distinctive responses to economic change of particular ethnic groups? This question is most easily answered for Hispanic families (although the specific causal connection has yet to be systematically shown). A recent U.S. Census report documents the flood over this period of poor immigrant families across the border from Mexico. Many of them have young children, and they have come in numbers great enough to be reflected in national statistics.[9]

- For this and other ethnic groups, there are also other forces at work.

FIGURE 5–7

POOR FAMILIES ARE GETTING POORER

Deficit in Income for Families in Poverty

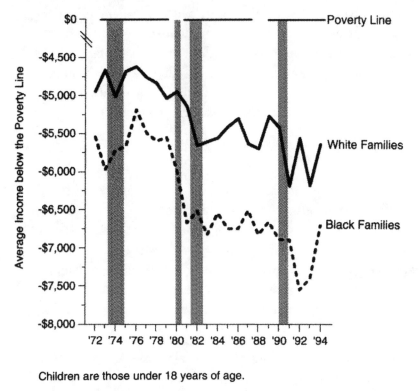

Children are those under 18 years of age.

- For more than two decades, the U.S. Bureau of the Census has included in its annual report on poverty a table documenting the extent to which the average income actually received by a particular group of families or individuals living in poverty falls short of the poverty threshold (the level of income deemed adequate to meet the basic needs for food, medical care, and a place to live).

- In 1972, poor black families with children under age 18 had to subsist on an average cash income (in 1994 constant dollars) that was about $5,500 below the amount judged sufficient to meet the needs of a family at that time, based on U.S. government standards. Today that average deficit has grown to $6,500 per year in current dollars.

• Although poor white families are less disadvantaged, they also cope with a significant and growing loss in income—from close to $5,000 per year in 1972 to $5,500 today.

• The gap between the two ethnic groups in lost annual income has grown substantially over the period of slowed economic growth.

• As one might expect, families with incomes well below the poverty line are especially affected by short-term economic recessions, with the impact being greater for groups with higher deficits—in this instance, for blacks more than for whites.

• The next two figures describe one of the main reasons that the incomes of poor families with young children have been going down.

FIGURE 5–8

GOVERNMENT BENEFITS HAVE BEEN DROPPING

Average Monthly AFDC Payment per Family

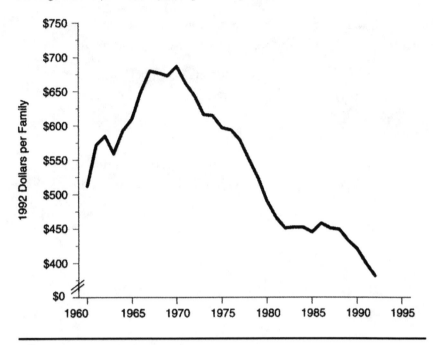

- For families whose financial resources are so low as to place them below the poverty line, their principal source of income is Aid to Families with Dependent Children (AFDC). This major source of financial support underwent a sharp reversal just when it was needed most.

- Children in poverty benefited as AFDC payments increased steadily through the 1950s and 1960s when economic growth was high, but then poor families lost ground at about the same rate as AFDC payments were reduced during the subsequent period of declining growth.

- Food stamps, which today add about $80 per month to the poor family's budget, have followed the same trend. About 60% of poor families with children, typically those with the greatest health and financial needs, receive this additional benefit.

• A recent special census report estimates the effect on the poverty rate of treating as taxable income the monetary equivalent of food stamps and other government cash and noncash benefits.[10] Requiring recipients to pay federal taxes on such benefits necessarily reduces available family income, often to a degree that places the family below the poverty threshold. For example, in 1993 the poverty rate for families with children under age 6 was 25.6%. Having to pay taxes on the value of government transfers (such as food stamps) would raise the poverty level to 28.6%. This means an increase in the number of young children living in poverty from 5.5 million to 6.6 million. Moreover, the families of these 6.6 million would have to cope with incomes even further below the poverty threshold, and with reduced accessibility to and benefits from AFDC and other government programs.

FIGURE 5-9

NUMBER OF FAMILIES NEEDING CASH ASSISTANCE IS GROWING

Children Under Age 18 Receiving AFDC Payments

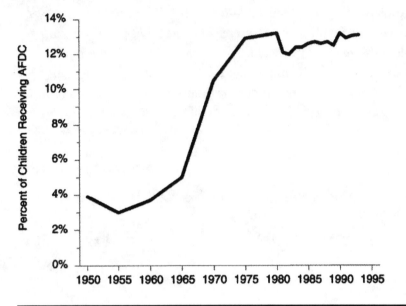

- Although the value of AFDC benefits in constant dollars has fallen sharply since the early 1970s, the number of needy families grew rapidly in the 1960s and 1970s, then leveled off in the late 1980s. As a result of recent legislation, the number threatens to go still higher.

- Does this mean that parents with young children are choosing to live on welfare rather than go to work?

FIGURE 5–10

**ALMOST TWO-THIRDS OF
POOR YOUNG CHILDREN
LIVE IN FAMILIES WITH
A WORKING ADULT**

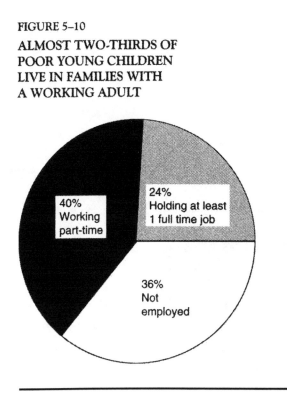

- More than 60% of families with young children have at least one adult family member working. About 90% of the time, that working adult is the child's parent.

FIGURE 5–11

LESS THAN ONE-THIRD OF POOR FAMILIES RELY EXCLUSIVELY ON WELFARE

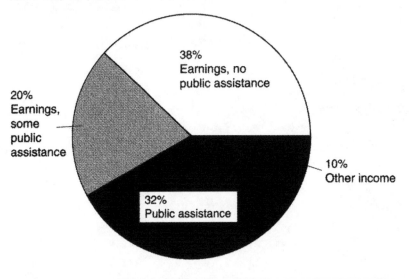

- Most poor families do not rely exclusively on welfare. The majority either rely exclusively on earnings or combine work and public assistance. In fact, the largest group of poor families are those with income only from jobs, without any public assistance.

- It is clear from this figure and the preceding one that, faced with declining resources, most poor families with young children are trying to make it on their own.

FIGURE 5–12

GOVERNMENT ASSISTANCE: FAMILIES WITH THE YOUNGEST CHILDREN BENEFIT THE LEAST

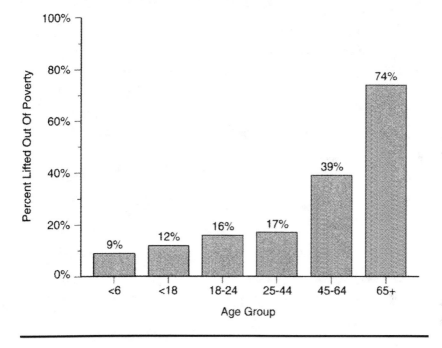

- This figure puts the whole story in perspective by documenting our current national priorities. Young children are at the bottom.

- The figures that follow tell about the lowest of the low—children growing up in poor single-mother families.

FIGURE 5-13

SINGLE PARENTHOOD AND POVERTY

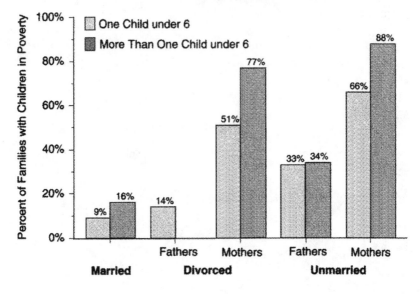

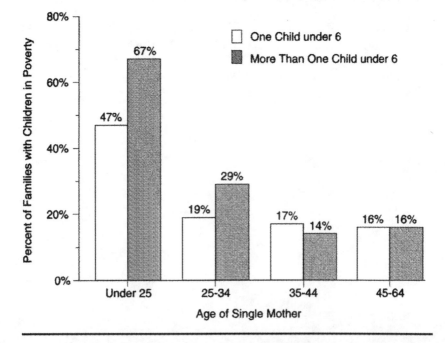

- Although government benefits provided to families in poverty are systematically greater for single-parent than for two-parent households, the percentage of young children growing up poor in single-parent families is much higher than that for youngsters in a home with two parents.

- Poverty rates are especially high for young children growing up with an unmarried single-parent mother.

- These risks are maximized when the mother is young and has more than one child.

- It is instructive to examine how these differences by family structure have changed over time and to do so separately for young children in black families and white families.

FIGURE 5–14

ONE- AND TWO-PARENT FAMILIES IN POVERTY

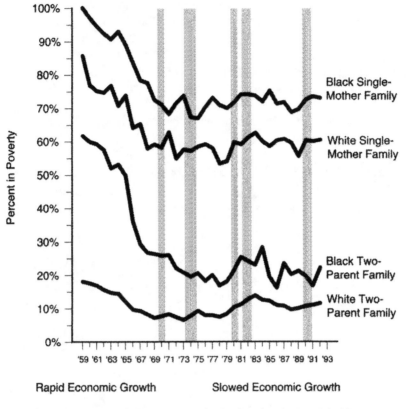

Rapid Economic Growth   Slowed Economic Growth

Sample consists of all children under 6 related to the householder.

- In general, whether economic growth was fast or slow, children in single-parent families have been at much greater risk of growing up poor.

- Black families and white families, both single and married, appear to have benefited from the more favorable economic conditions prevailing from the 1960s to the early 1970s.

- Taken as a whole, the findings on changes over time in poverty rates for families with young children would seem to contradict some well-established facts. Unlike all prior figures for poverty rates (see

Figures 5–3, 5–4, and 5–6), this figure fails to show a marked increase in poverty for all groups during the period of slowed economic growth beginning in the mid-1970s and continuing up to the present. To put the paradox more pointedly, if, during this time, poverty rates are not rising significantly for any of these four groups, how can more families with young children be once again falling into poverty?

• This figure provides the key for resolving this discrepancy. Once ethnic groups are compared within the same family structures, the previously documented wide gap in poverty rates for black children is substantially reduced. How does this come about?

FIGURE 5-15

THE MORE SINGLE MOTHERS, THE MORE POVERTY

Distribution of Young Children in Poverty by State of the Economy

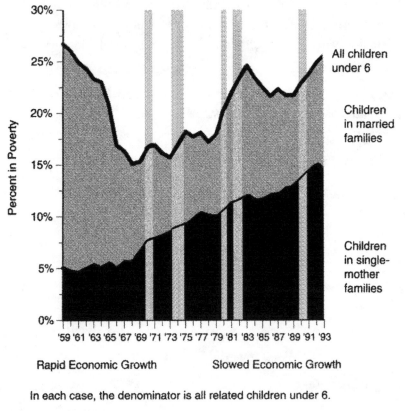

In each case, the denominator is all related children under 6.

This is a cumulative graph.

- During the period of rapid economic growth, the proportion of married families with young children fell sharply but remained fairly constant thereafter except during periods of economic recession and recovery.

- By contrast, the proportion of single-mother families in poverty increased steadily through the successive periods of rapid and slowed economic growth.

- We already know that the poverty rate for both single-mother and two-parent families within each ethnic group remained relatively unchanged during the period of weaker economic growth. We also know that the overall poverty rate for single-mother families is substantially higher than that for two-parent households. It follows that the rising poverty rate for all children under age 6 in the period of slowed economic growth during the past two decades is attributable primarily to the increasing number of youngsters living in poor single-mother families.

• The next graph brings the argument home.

FIGURE 5–16

AMONG THE POOR, MORE YOUNG CHILDREN HAVE BEEN GROWING UP IN SINGLE-MOTHER FAMILIES

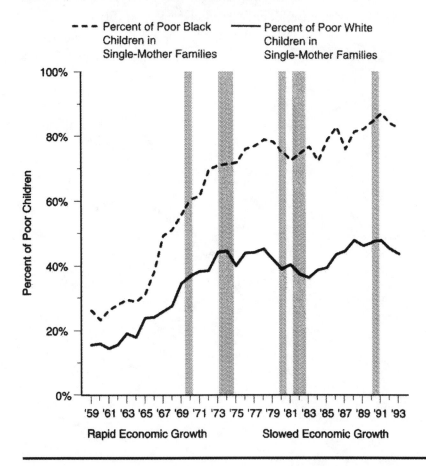

- This dramatic social change for both black and white families over the course of four decades has been called the feminization of poverty.

- The greatest increase in poor single-mother families occurred during a period of rapid economic growth rather than in the subsequent less favorable economic climate. This contrast suggests that the observed trend, although affected by periods of recession (particularly in the case of black single-mother families), is not primarily driven by the state of the national economy.

- As the proportion of young children living in single-parent families increases, that for children in two-parent families must necessarily decline.[11] It is instructive to restate the relationship:

  - Most young, poor black children used to live with two parents; today more than 80% live with only one.
  - Over 80% of poor white children used to live with two parents; today almost half live with only one.

- To return to the paradoxical findings, when the analysis presented in the preceding figure is repeated separately for blacks and whites, it reveals the same kind of result: since 1979, neither group has fallen back into poverty. However, because the proportion of single-mother families among the poor has risen so sharply, especially for blacks, the overall poverty rate for young black children has increased even more than it has for whites.

FIGURE 5-17

THE MORE POVERTY, THE MORE SINGLE PARENTHOOD

Divorced and Unmarried Motherhood, by Race and Childhood Poverty Status

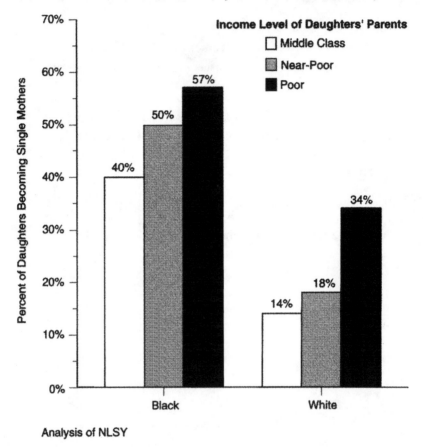

Analysis of NLSY

- Women who have grown up in poverty are more likely than those from middle-class backgrounds to become single parents.[12]

- This risk is especially high for women growing up in poor, black families.

- When the findings from the preceding figures are considered together, they lead to a consequential conclusion: single parenthood and poverty are a two-way street, with the disruptive effects of each reinforcing the other.

• This conclusion is supported by other research evidence, some of it presented in the preceding chapter. For example, growing up in poverty markedly increases the risks associated with being raised by a single parent in terms of developmental outcomes like the following: dropping out of school or college, score on the AFQT test, or becoming a teenaged mother. To look at the same joint effect from the opposite direction, there is poverty itself. Adult children of poor single-parent mothers were much more likely to end up in poverty themselves than were those from middle-class single-parent homes, especially if their own mother had never married. In sum, these were children whose competence and well-being as adults had been placed at more than double jeopardy early in their lives.

• Single parenthood is not the only street on which poverty walks in both directions.

FIGURE 5–18

THE MORE EDUCATION, THE LESS POVERTY

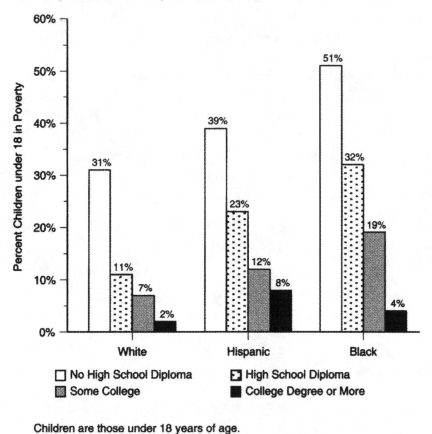

Children are those under 18 years of age.

• One of the more disturbing findings reported in the preceding chapter was the high risk of dropping out of school for children growing up in poverty, especially for those raised by a single-parent mother. In short, the more poverty, the less education—once again across generations.

• This figure looks at it the other way around and tells a different story:

  • Today, in a period of slow economic growth, education constitutes a powerful force in decreasing the risk that a family will end up in poverty, with completion of high school by the child's parent being an especially critical factor.[13]

- The effect is substantial for all three of the nation's largest ethnic groups: whites, Hispanics, and blacks.

- This finding takes on added significance in the light of evidence presented in the next chapter that documents corresponding gains in school achievement by black students, in part because their parents have received more education.

- The critical issue is whether the gains that can be obtained through improving education can withstand, let alone overcome, the mutually reinforcing, developmentally disruptive effects of growing up in a poor single-parent family in the United States today.

FIGURE 5–19

POVERTY ACROSS GENERATIONS:
GENDER MAKES A DIFFERENCE

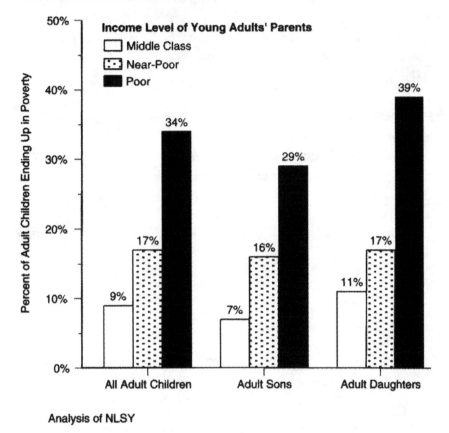

Analysis of NLSY

- Children who grew up in a poor family were, as young adults, more than three times as likely to end up in poverty themselves than were their age-mates from middle-class backgrounds.

- The odds were even higher for young adults raised in black families, with Hispanics falling in between. These findings are consistent with the stronger joint effects of poverty and single parenthood in black than in white families.[14]

- The recurrence of poverty across generations was higher for women than for young men. This finding takes on special significance given two additional facts: percentage of single-parent mothers has been rising, especially among families in poverty, and it is primarily women rather than men who bring up the next generation, especially in its early years.

• The finding that the risk of poverty across generations was higher for females stands in contrast to an opposite pattern for males. Boys growing up in poor families were more likely than girls to drop out of school. Taken together, these findings reflect the differential vulnerability to developmental stress observed in males and females.

• The final two figures in this chapter contain its most sobering message.

FIGURE 5-20
AMERICA'S CHILDREN IN DEEP POVERTY

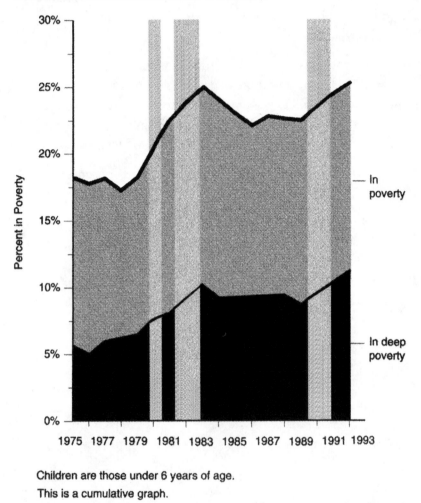

Children are those under 6 years of age.
This is a cumulative graph.

• Every year since the late 1970s, the U.S. Census has published data
on the number of children living in families 50% below the poverty
line. According to federal statistics, their income was only half of
what a family of a given size requires to meet basic expenses for food,
housing, and other living costs. This also means that the families in
this group have only half the income that would already have qualified them to receive public assistance. In 1994, a family consisting of

two adults and two children under age 18 and falling in this category would have had an annual income of no more than $7,514; the corresponding figure for a single mother with one child under 18 was $5,964 per year.

- Over the past two decades, the percentage of children living in such deep poverty has more than doubled, from 1.1 million in 1975 to 2.8 million in 1994. Today they account for 47% of all young children in poverty, as compared with a third, 32%, in 1975, just before the rapid decline in economic growth.

- The percentage of young white children in deep poverty today is somewhat lower than that for all children under age 6 (7.7% versus 8.2%), but the corresponding figure for black youngsters is much higher. Since economic growth began to decline in the late 1970s, this percentage has been rising at a faster rate than that for whites. Today one-third of all black children under age 6 are living in deep poverty.

- With respect to poor white children, there is yet another reality that must be confronted.

FIGURE 5–21

MOST YOUNG CHILDREN LIVING IN POVERTY ARE WHITE

Distribution of Poor Children by Race and Family Structure

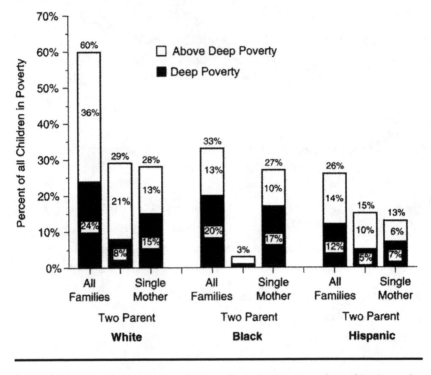

- Of all children in poverty, almost a quarter live in white families who are in deep poverty. For children in white families, the figure for those growing up poor but not in deep poverty is 36%.

- The most general finding revealed by the figure is stated in its title. But there are also some noteworthy exceptions to this overall trend.

- The statement applies to poor children in families above deep poverty but not to all those within it. Specifically, compared to whites, today there are at least as many, if not more, black youngsters growing up in single-mother families in deep poverty.

- Particularly striking is the low percentage, both within deep poverty and above it, of black children under age 6 living with two parents. Of all young children living below the poverty line, only 3% are growing up in black two-parent families, who make up 18% of all poor black children. Does this mean that more two-parent families are moving up and out of poverty? Hardly likely, for two reasons. First, single parenthood is increasing among all black families, rich and poor, even faster than among all whites. Second, comparable census data are available for 1975, just at the end of the period of rapid economic growth. At that time, the percentage of white two-parent families was 18%—higher than it is today. And at that time, white single-mother families in poverty still exceeded black.

• The main reason for the predominance of white families among the poor is that whites constitute the overwhelming majority of the population. At the same time, on a percentage basis, white families as a whole are not experiencing the extent of poverty endured by America's major—and many minor—minorities. At least, not yet.

LOOKING TO THE FUTURE

Neither poverty nor the forces that produce it represents a steady state. Rather, they constitute a dynamic system of converging, mutually reinforcing processes taking place over time, with both short-term fluctuations and longer-term trajectories with a momentum of their own. Some groups in society are more vulnerable to these escalating forces, others less so, but all are moving in the same direction.

Single parenthood, which thrived during a period of strong economic growth, ultimately became a producer of poverty and a product of it. Correspondingly, the proportion in poverty today of young children of white single-parent mothers (43%) is about the same as had already been reached by black single-parent mothers in the late 1960s.

But there is even more at stake. The same forces of disarray that lead to family poverty also have substantial impact on the majority of the country's children who are growing up in more favorable economic circumstances. We turn to the context that, next to the family, exerts the greatest influence on the competence and character of the next generation of Americans: schools.

6

AMERICAN EDUCATION

Looking Inward and Outward

There exists a connection between a family's economic resources and a child's school performance; children from the most economically disadvantaged families tend to have the lowest SAT scores, the lowest achievement test scores, and the highest dropout rates from high school. And children with the lowest SATs and school achievement scores are more likely to end up in poverty as adults. As test scores plummetted throughout the past thirty years, so did income. Children from families in poverty tend to have far lower SATs than those from affluent families. The combined SATs of children whose parents earn over $70,000 a year are, on average, 200 points higher (531 math, 469 verbal) than those of children whose families earn between $10,000 and $20,000 (435 math, 377 verbal). All of this implies an intergenerational cycle of poverty given substance by the steady, prolonged decrement in test scores and concomitant decline in real wages.

Finally, after a long period of steady decline, American students' test score performance has begun to show an upturn. Although this upturn is not large, it does break the general pattern of decline that has been evident since the 1960s. Of interest in this chapter is that the biggest gains have been made by the most disadvantaged students. A number of factors have been implicated in this improvement in achievement test scores, including smaller family sizes, hence greater income per child, greater educational spending targeted to programs serving disadvantaged children, desegregation of some inner-city schools, and increases in parental educational attainment.

While test scores have risen dramatically for some groups and slightly for others, they have remained stagnant for still others. As a result, when all groups are combined, there is a small gain overall, while our international trading partners' children have made large gains. Thus, on international comparisons, American students have fallen below average in terms of their relative ranking. Even the test scores of the top American students have fallen behind those of major U.S. trading partners, so the problem is not confined to inner-city schools. In fact, about half of all two- and four-year college graduates operate at a fairly low level on tests of mathematical and verbal literacy.

In this chapter, we explore some of these trends and discuss their implications for America in the next century.

FIGURE 6–1

AVERAGE GROWTH IN TEST SCORES 1971–1990

American Students

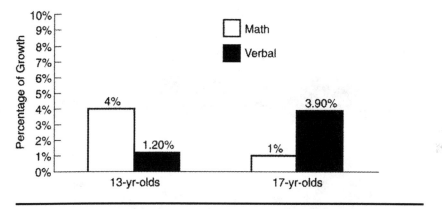

- Students' verbal and mathematical achievement test scores are slightly higher today than they were in the early 1970s.

- Students scored higher on math and verbal/reading tests in 1990 than their predecessors did in 1971–1973. For example, 17 year olds in 1990 scored approximately 3.9 percentage points higher on verbal reasoning tasks than 17 year olds did in 1971, and 14 year olds scored 4 percentage points higher on math tasks in 1990 than was true of their predecessors in 1971.

- These are not huge gains, but they do fly in the face of the oft-reported downward slide in educational scores.

FIGURE 6–2

CHANGES IN AMERICAN STUDENTS' ACHIEVEMENT SCORES, 1973–1990

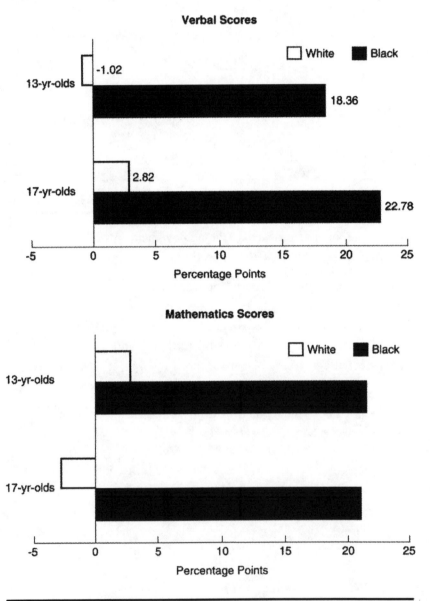

Verbal Scores

Mathematics Scores

- Within the overall gains in educational test scores, there is great racial diversity, with the largest gains being made by black students.

- Nearly all of the upward gain of the past twenty years has been due to the extremely large gains made by black 13 and 17 year olds. Changes in the test scores of white students over this same period have been minimal—between plus or minus 4 percentage points.

- At the time that the first *National Assessment of Educational Progress* (NAEP) results were reported twenty years ago, black students' average achievement scores were 35 to 40 percentage points below those of white students. Today the average black student has gained between 18 and 25 points, thus cutting the black–white differential in half, to approximately 17 to 25 points, depending on the test.

- There is no generally agreed on cause of the slight drop in white 13 year olds' verbal scores over this period or of white 17 year olds' slight decline in math scores.

FIGURE 6–3

GROWTH IN COLLEGE GRADUATES
AMONG PARENTS OF ADOLESCENTS, 1973–1990

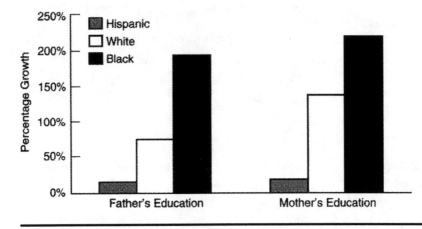

- Several factors are commonly cited as helping to narrow the black-white difference in test scores:

  - Educational spending is up over 250% in real dollars during this time period, with increases in spending disproportionately targeted to programs serving minority youngsters (e.g., Title 1, Head Start, lunch programs).

  - Parental educational attainment, which is linked to children's educational attainment, went up markedly between 1970 and 1990. Gains in educational attainment of parents were far more pronounced for black families than for white and Hispanic families. For example, black mothers' rate of college completion increased far faster than white or Hispanic parents' during this period: approximately 200% for blacks versus 120% for whites and 25% for Hispanics. Similarly, the rate of attending at least some college grew by approximately 354% for black mothers versus 81% for white mothers and 24% for Hispanic mothers. At all levels, the educational attainment of black parents grew faster than that of white and Hispanic parents.

  - Real income per child has gone up in all families but particularly in black families, even while poverty rates for young children also have increased. This is because the average family size for nonwelfare families has dropped dramatically during the past two decades, thus resulting in greater income per child in these families.

• Many traditional black schools have been desegregated, a factor known to be associated with rising test scores of minority youngsters.

FIGURE 6–4

AVERAGE DIFFERENCES IN
AMERICAN STUDENTS' VERBAL TEST SCORES, 1990

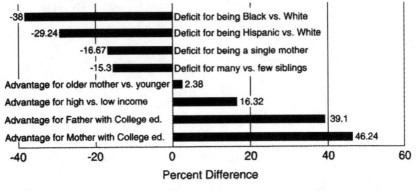

Percent Difference

- Despite their large gains, black students still score well below white youngsters. Hispanic youngsters score between blacks and whites in terms of gains. Even after adjustment for income, number of siblings, mother's age at birth, and both parents' educational levels, black and Hispanic students continue to lag between 15 and 20 points behind white students, and they rarely attain the highest achievement status on tests of math and reading.

- A number of factors have effects on children's *verbal* test scores:

  - The difference between having a mother with a college education versus one with less than a high school diploma is roughly 46 points (which translates into a 20% gap on a test of verbal reasoning).
  - The difference between a parent who earns over $40,000 per year versus only $15,000 per year is approximately 16 points (around a 7% difference).

- The difference between blacks and whites is 38 points (roughly 17%); approximately 29 points separate Hispanics and whites (this translates to a gap of 13%). Similar results are found for *math* scores. All of this may seem like a further discussion of the baleful effects of being from a single-parent family that have been chronicled, but the picture gets more complicated (and interesting).

FIGURE 6–5

MEAN DIFFERENCES IN AMERICAN STUDENTS' VERBAL TEST SCORES AFTER ADJUSTMENT, 1990

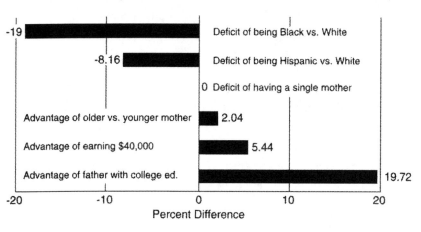

- Test scores fluctuate with family structure, with evidence suggesting that children of single mothers do worse than those from two-parent families; however, this difference appears to be due largely, if not entirely, to variations in income and education rather than to differences in family structure per se.

- The gap between children of single and married mothers (16.67 points on tests of verbal reasoning and similar differences on tests of mathematical reasoning) is totally eliminated when educational and economic factors are taken into account. Specifically, children of single-mothers who possess comparable educational and economic resources to those found in two-parent families perform within a single point of children from two-parent families on tests of mathematics, and identically to such children on tests of verbal reasoning.

- Controlling for differences in a variety of background factors on children's test scores shows what differences we should expect to be associated with a single factor (race, single parenthood, age of mother at time of child's birth, earning over $40,000 annually versus earning under $15,000, and parental educational level) when all of the other factors are equated. For instance, the 38-point gap associated with being black is cut in half when families are equated on all other factors (income, parental education, etc.). Thus, when we take into account differences in income and education, the gaps in verbal scores seen in Figure 6–4 are cut in half, and the gap associated with being a single mother is completely eliminated. A similar result is found for differences in math scores of single versus two-parent families.

- While increments in parents' educational level are associated with increases in their offspring's test scores, this effect is especially pronounced for parents at the lowest end. Another way of saying this is that increases in earnings and education make a bigger difference for poor parents than they do for wealthy ones.

- That children from single-parent families who have access to the same educational and economic resources as found among two-parent families do as well as students in two-parent families, runs counter to the intuition that single-parent families are inherently deleterious to children's educational achievement. But the empirical reality is that most single-parent families are poor; thus their children do not usually do as well. So, a disproportionately large segment of single-parent families do *not* possess equal education and income to those of two-parent families.

- It appears that mother's and father's educational attainment—here dichotomized as finishing college versus failure to complete high school—is the single biggest factor in determining children's educational success. Children whose parents are college graduates score 18 to 20 points above children of non–high-school graduates on math and verbal tests, even after taking into consideration differences in income, number of siblings in the home, race, and so forth.

- That children of single mothers do as well as the children of two-parent families when consideration is given to family background factors that tend to be correlated with being a single parent needs to be kept in mind when thinking about solutions to educational problems; failure to take them into account could mislead the reader into thinking that some factors are causative when they may not be.

• Policies to ameliorate single parenthood might not boost test scores if mothers continue to possess a lack of education and limited income. This renders the results in Figure 6–4 deceptively simplistic when the appropriate statistical controls are made in Figure 6–5. What Figure 6–5 does not show, however, is that the effect of added income and education is greatest among families that possess the least money and education, and the effects are least among families that are already wealthy.

• These analyses reveal where America can have its greatest impact on student achievement: if single mothers were encouraged to continue their own education following pregnancy, this alone would be expected to reduce significantly the deficit of children from single-parent families.

FIGURE 6–6

INTERNATIONAL COMPARISONS OF MATH ACHIEVEMENT

(A) Fourth Graders; (B) Eighth Graders; (C) Seniors Taking Calculus

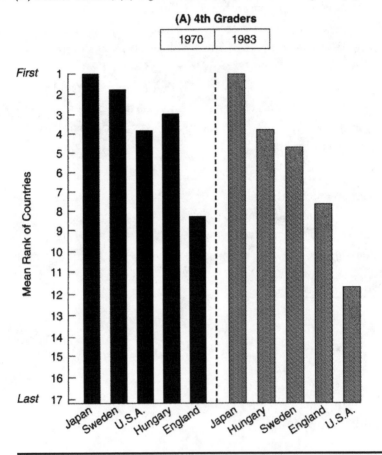

- On international comparisons, there has been a sizable drop in the relative ranking of American students' test scores in mathematics and science. Our children have gone from the middle of the international pack to near the bottom.

- At the same time that black children have made substantial progress in closing the racial gap in America, the test scores of white children have remained stagnant. This has allowed the test scores of our major trading partners' children to overtake those of our own children.

FIGURE 6–6 CONT'D

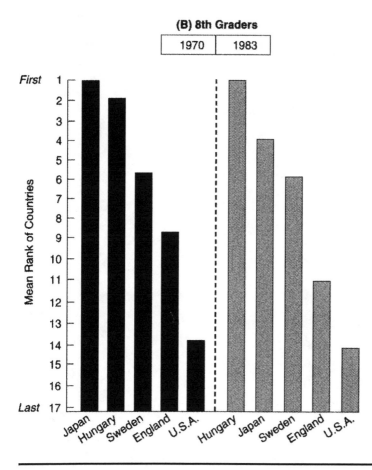

(B) 8th Graders

| 1970 | 1983 |

• Between the late 1960s and the early 1990s approximately twenty nations have participated in international comparative assessments on science, math, and literacy. If one can draw a single generalization from these data series, it is this: While America does very well on literacy (usually ranking second behind only Finland), it does poorly in all areas of science and math. Often American students score at or below the median of all countries, despite our high per-pupil expenditures.

• American fourth-graders ranked fourth among countries tested in 1970 but had dropped to twelfth place by the mid-1980s. The picture for American eighth graders is even worse; they were near the

FIGURE 6–6 CONT'D

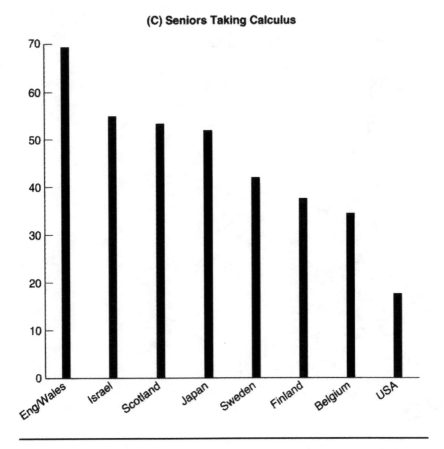

(C) Seniors Taking Calculus

bottom of the international rankings in 1970 (fifteenth out of seventeen), and they have remained there. The problems cannot be dismissed as those of inner-city youths' scoring well below average; the U.S. scores lowest on international tests of calculus, in general achieving less than half of the children of its major trading partners.

- Generally on international assessments, American children tested in the early grades do better than those tested in later grades. This trend repeats itself frequently; that is, American students seem to lose ground in relation to their international peers the longer they are in school, as seen with the drop-off in scores between the fourth-grade and eighth grade.

FIGURE 6–7

**INTERNATIONAL COMPARISONS
OF HIGH SCHOOL SENIORS, 1990**

Raw Scores of Twelfth Graders on Math and Science Achievement Tests

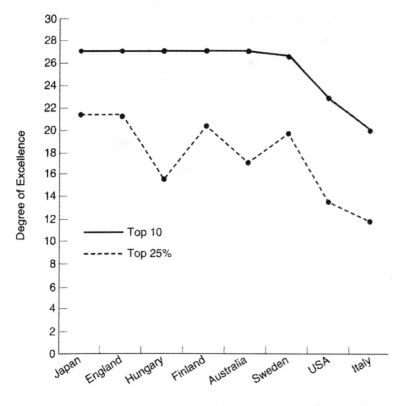

• America can boast, along with Japan and Germany, the highest re-
tention rates in the world: 87% of the children who begin first grade
receive a high school diploma or general equivalency diploma by the
age of 30, and American students have the highest rate of enrolling
in postsecondary institutions, nearly doubling the rates of those of
U.S. international trading partners.[1] Nevertheless, there are areas of
grave concern when we shift from measures of graduation and ma-
triculation to measures of how much students are actually learning.

• There are startling gaps in even the best students' knowledge when
they are compared to students from other countries. In interna-

tional comparisons of the top 10% and top 25% of students (this group is considered the raw material for the next generation's political leaders, science and engineering elite, and business managers), American students tend to be nearer the achievement levels of Italy and Thailand in such comparisons than to Japan, Sweden, and England.

FIGURE 6–8

PERCENTAGE OF 9 YEAR OLDS WHO REPORT WATCHING
OVER 5 HOURS OF TELEVISION PER WEEKDAY

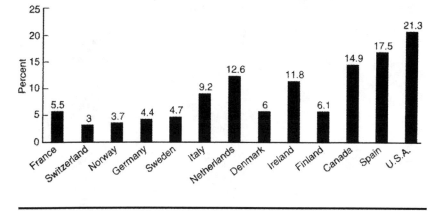

- The reason for the gap in U.S. students' achievement is not clear. One of numerous possibilities is the heavy television viewing by American youth. Twenty-one percent of American youth watch five or more hours of television on school nights, far more than the children of U.S. trading partners.

- There is a correlation between television viewing and school performance: the more a child watches television, the lower his or her grades tend to be. But the negative correlation between heavy television viewing and test scores might be the result of some third variable, such as social class (e.g., heavier television viewing is more commonly found among poor children; television viewing of middle-class children might involve more educational programs and be accompanied by didactic parental supervision). At this point, all one can say with confidence is that children spending five or more hours in front of a television set on school nights are actually spending more time in that context than they are in school itself.

FIGURE 6–9

**TIME THAT NO ONE WAS LEADING INSTRUCTION
IN FIRST AND FIFTH GRADES**

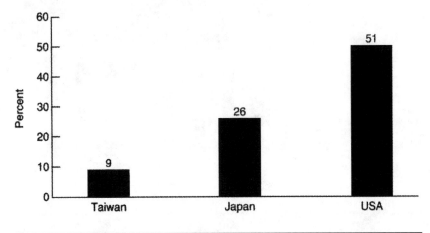

- Another possible factor in America's decline on international rankings is the differential manner in which education is delivered. Numerous commentators have remarked that American teachers spend disproportionately more of their instructional day keeping order in the classroom, and as a result children spend far more of their school day in self-directed activities than in teacher-directed ones.

- Compared to Japanese and Chinese classrooms in one study, American youngsters spend much more of their time in activities that are not under the direct guidance of their teacher.[2]

FIGURE 6–10

RESULTS OF THE 1992 NATIONAL ADULT LITERACY STUDY

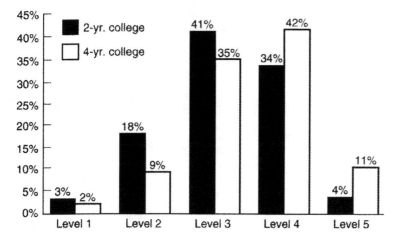

Example of Level 4 Quantitative Literacy is: Estimate the cost per ounce of creamy peanut butter if the price is $1.99 for 20 ounces (Unit Price= $1.59 per lb.). Example of Level 5 Quantitative Literacy is: What is the total amount of interest charges you'd pay if you borrowed $10,000 at 14.25% Annual Percentage Rate, which translates into 120 monthly payments of $156.77.

- In addition to the problems facing elementary and secondary education in America, there are portentous signs suggesting that higher education is not meeting expectations. College graduates no longer have the skills they were once assumed to possess.

- The achievement levels of college graduates (from both two- and four-year institutions of higher learning) are embarrassingly low. In 1992, approximately half of all college graduates were classified as "level 3 or lower" on a survey of 26,000 adults who were asked to solve everyday problems, such as reading an editorial and answering questions. Levels 4 and 5 were not achieved by half of all graduates. These included such problems as calculating the amount of interest due on a loan.

- During the past fifteen years, there has been a significant change in the proportion of low-achieving high school students who have shifted out of vocational and general education programs into college-preparation programs. In the 1980s, there was a 98% increase in the number of low-achieving students who enrolled in these programs, according to data provided by the U.S. Department of Education. (Various explanations for this shift have been put forward, including the perception among students and their parents that vocational and general education programs were dead-end streets and that a college degree was a ticket to prosperity.) Putting aside the reason for the huge shift into college-preparation programs, it is clear that many more ill-prepared high school students are now attending college. This helps explain the finding that half of all college graduates are operating on a low level.

LOOKING TO THE FUTURE

Numerous commentators have remarked that today's students are ill equipped to perform many of the functions required in modern (computerized) workplaces. It has become common for companies like Westinghouse and General Motors to develop extensive and costly training programs to inculcate skills that were once assumed to have been attained by high school graduates (e.g., training a shipping clerk to convert pounds to kilograms). And recently, James W. Hayes, in a national address to the Cleveland Forum on National Public Radio, noted that the most important question business leaders ask when they are scouting a location for a new plant is what the educational level of the workforce is, expressing dissatisfaction with the skills of the typical worker.[3]

Notwithstanding the costs associated with such industry-financed training in basic skills, there is a second set of consequences of low achievement scores: substantial evidence exists that at all levels of achievement, those who have completed more schooling earn more money and are employed more weeks than are their less-educated peers. For example, college graduates who score in the highest literacy level earn approximately 33% more than high school graduates who score in the very same literacy level, and the same is true of college graduates at every other skill level; they outearn their high school counterparts at the comparable skill level (Figure 6–11). Moreover, at any given level of schooling attained (e.g., among high school students only), higher levels of achievement are associated with higher earnings and more weeks employed.

Both educational attainment (highest grade completed) and achievement levels within grades appear to have consequences not only for America's industrial efficiency but also for the economic health of the individual workers themselves. According to the latest census data, the average high school dropout can expect to earn only $12,809 per year, while the average high school graduate can expect to earn $18,737, the average college graduate can expect to earn $32,629, the average holder of a master's degree can expect to earn $40,368, the average holder of a doctoral degree can expect to earn $54,904, and the

FIGURE 6–11

WEEKLY WAGES, BY LITERACY LEVEL

United States, 1992

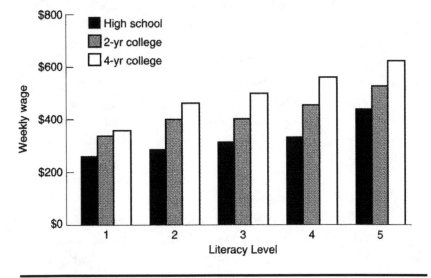

average holder of a professional degree can expect to earn $74,560.[4]
Over the course of their lifetimes, high school dropouts can expect to earn
$212,000 less than high school graduates, $812,000 less than college graduates, and $2,404,000 less than persons with professional degrees.

Are there any solutions that suggest themselves? A point made earlier deserves reiterating: spending more money in the past twenty years
has paid off for minority youngsters, who closed half the gap in their
test scores in relation to white students. But spending has leveled off in
the past few years in real dollars, and it is unlikely to increase in the
coming decade. Yet, even if increased funding were financially possible
and politically palatable, it might not be sufficient in and of itself to
stem the downward tide of American students on international comparisons. This is because there is no strong relationship in the vast majority of schools in industrial countries between average student expenditures (e.g., teacher salary, costs of labs/books) and test score
outcomes.[5] Schools that are above a certain minimum standard of
safety and health are unlikely to improve their students' test scores

merely by increasing teacher salaries, spending more on books, and so forth. The one area where there *is* a demonstrable benefit associated with increased spending is reducing class size.[6] It has been shown that reducing class size by 35% in the elementary school grades is associated with approximately a .25 standard deviation gain on test scores (e.g., a gain equivalent to increasing reading test scores from the fiftieth percentile to the sixtieth percentile). Furthermore, the magnitude of the gain associated with being in a smaller classroom is nearly double for minority children, for the first two years of school only. After that, there is no difference in gains between different racial groups. In the coming decade, America will have to decide whether the magnitude of such gains outweighs the advantages of expenditures for other societal goals.

7

CHANGING AGE TRENDS

The Pyramid Upside Down?[1]

The trends and social forces described throughout this book are occurring in the context of an aging population that is dramatically transforming America. Changes in life expectancy and in fertility are recasting the age distribution of Americans, creating both challenges and opportunities for older people and for the nation.

The trends documented in the preceding chapters are played out in the later years of adulthood through the process of a cumulation of advantage or disadvantage. Thus, widening income inequality in the prime years of adulthood means that many come to their later years without the security of savings, an adequate pension, or a home that is paid for. For others, however, old age becomes a time to reap the liberal retirement benefits of the American dream accruing after a lifetime of steady employment and pension investment.

There is also an interdependency between generations as well as between beliefs and behavior at different stages of the life course. For example, today's youth who feel that they cannot trust people are likely to grow old with similar views and to transmit these suspicions about individuals and groups to their own children. Interdependency is also reflected in educational attainment; today's young adults who are functionally illiterate are ill equipped to face the challenges of aging or to prepare their children for a society where education and training are the tickets to stable, secure employment. This translates to a cumulation of disadvantage, with those less fortunate in educational and occupational opportunities throughout their lives having fewer psychological, social, and economic resources to deal with the realities of growing old or to pass on to their children and grandchildren.

As we have seen, for many Americans education provides a pathway to the American dream of lifelong employment with advances along a career ladder or, at least, wage increases in tandem with increases in seniority. Education also is often a passport to good health. Wide-scale advances in educational attainment and health will reshape our notions about old age and older people as unprecedented numbers of Americans enter later adulthood with greater knowledge, insights, and skills, also reflected in lifestyle choices (regarding nutrition, exercise, smoking, for example) that promote health and vigor.

Notions of the interdependency of the two halves of the life course and the cumulation of advantage and disadvantage imply continuity; that is, early character and competence, along with early experiences, choices, and resources, affect life chances and life quality in the later years. But growing older also represents a time of change. Old age often brings major life transitions: the onset of disability for self or spouse, leaving one's job, widowhood, caregiving for older (and younger) kin. These transitions represent key emotional turning points and often pose major economic and social dislocations as well. Older women are particularly at risk of economic hardship following widowhood, since most still rely on husbands' pensions and social security benefits. And with age Americans become more vulnerable to social isolation, which research shows can lead to depression, illness, and even death. Those who have not participated in religious, civic, or other voluntary organizations as youth and prime-age adults are particularly susceptible to even greater social disconnection as they age.

The interplay between beliefs and values, policies and practices in society at large, on the one hand, and families and individual lives, on the other, can be seen throughout this book and is particularly evident in old age. A lifetime of steady employment, the timing of retirement, the provision and costs of medical care and pensions, housing options and choices, the development of competence and character: all affect and are affected by individual abilities and preferences, cultural values and expectations, and the ways employers, governments, and communities structure opportunities and constraints. Most of our great-grandfathers, for example, did not have the luxury of retiring unless they were physically unable to continue to work. Most older Americans today, by contrast, are reaping the benefits of the social security system as well as the economic boom years of high-wage jobs that included economic security as a taken-for-granted benefit. Younger generations, however, are looking to their own futures with trepidation. Many find it hard to make ends meet, much less plan for their old age, while at the same time the federal government seeks to lower the safety net for the old, the poor, and the disadvantaged, and employers are less likely to provide liberal fringe benefits.

The information provided in this chapter points to a fundamental shift in the age distribution of the nation. America, always a youth-centered nation, is becoming old. Moreover, we see the heterogeneity of this population of older Americans, who differ by education, health, skills, and economic security, as well as by age, race, and gender. The fact is that older Americans increasingly look like what the preceding chapters have shown is true for the rest of the population: some are well off, some are poor, some are managing in between. As the economist James Schulz points out, this is a remarkable observation, since in the past the word *old* was often synonymous with *destitute*.[1] (Schulz, 1988). The economic sufficiency of most contemporary older Americans is a true American success story, especially for those retiring from career jobs with good pay and comfortable pensions. But is it a success story that will continue?

FIGURE 7–1

**AMERICA'S POPULATION IS AGING AND
IT IS PROJECTED TO GET OLDER**

Population over Age 65, 1900–2030

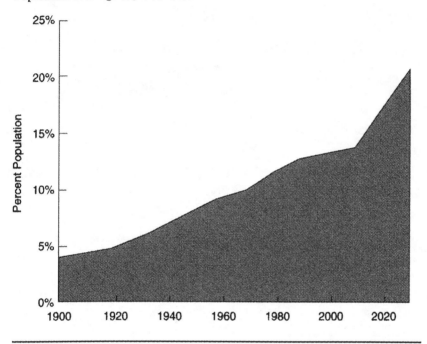

- We are experiencing unprecedented growth in both the numbers of older people and the proportion of the American population that is old, due to trends in longevity and fertility, as well as the aging of the baby boom generation (members of that very large cohort born during a period of high fertility after World War II, from 1946 to 1964).

- The proportion of older Americans has tripled in this century. While only one out of every twenty-five Americans (4%) was age 65 or older at the turn of this century, as we approach the next century one of every eight Americans (13%) is at least 65 years old. One in five (22%) Americans will be 65 or older by the year 2030.

FIGURE 7-2

**THE ABSOLUTE NUMBER OF OLDER AMERICANS
IS INCREASING EXPONENTIALLY, 1940–2080**

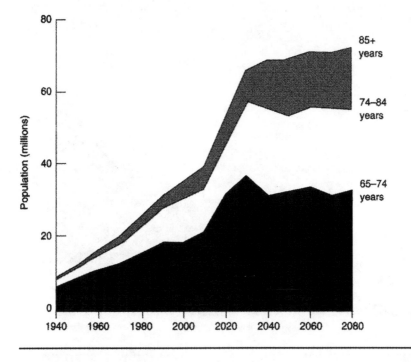

- America's population is not only aging; it is going to get even older. As the baby boomers enter old age, we will see a more than doubling of the elderly population. The number of Americans age 65 or older is projected to be close to 70 million by the year 2030, twice the number in this age group in 1990.

- The elderly population is becoming increasingly old, with the fastest-growing age group in the United States—growing six times faster than the rest of the population—the oldest of the old, those age 85 and over. Between 1960 and 1994 alone the number of these oldest old rose 274 percent.

- There are 3 million Americans age 85 or older. This number is striking when compared to the beginning of the twentieth century, when only 100,000 Americans were over age 85. As the baby boom generation moves into the ranks of the oldest old in the next century (2031), we can anticipate 19 million Americans at least 85 years of age.

FIGURE 7–3

**OLDER AMERICANS WILL SOON OUTNUMBER
CHILDREN UNDER 18, 1940–2080**

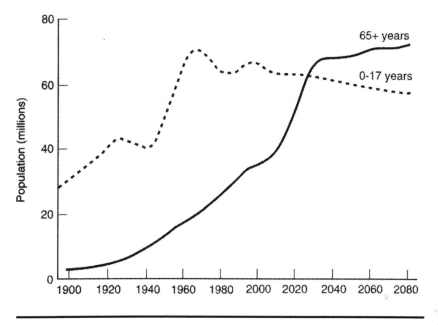

- America has always been a youth-centered society, with youth symbolizing energy, romance, promise. But no more.

- At the beginning of the twentieth century, the United States was a very young country, with a median age of only 23; that is, half of the population was 23 years old or younger. In 1990 the median age was 33; by 2030 it will be 42.

- In 1960, near the peak of the baby boom, more than one of every three Americans (36%) was a child under the age of 18 and less than one in ten (9%) was age 65 or older. During the 2020s about equal proportions will be under age 18 (21%) or over age 65 (20%). By the year 2030 there will be more Americans over 65 than there are children under 18.

FIGURE 7–4

**THE NEW AMERICAN WORKFORCE WILL REFLECT
NOT ONLY MORE WOMEN AND MINORITIES
BUT ALSO MORE OLDER WORKERS**

- The baby boomers have learned that there is life after 30; soon they will learn about life in later adulthood. The oldest baby boomers began turning 50 years old in 1996 and will begin reaching age 62 in the year 2008.

- These maturing baby boomers mean that the workforce is also maturing, as changes in its composition show.

- The Department of Labor estimates that by 2005 almost 30% of the working-age population will be 55 and older, a proportion that will climb to almost 40% by 2020.

FIGURE 7–5

INCREASING LIFE EXPECTANCY OF AMERICANS,
AT BIRTH AND OF THOSE LIVING TO AGE 65

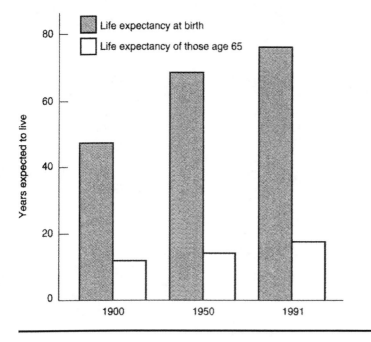

- Medical advances and lifestyle changes (such as better sanitation and nutrition) have resulted in a remarkable increase in life expectancy (the average number of years one can expect to live).

- At the nation's founding, life expectancy was 35 years. As we moved into the twentieth century, many Americans died in childhood or early adulthood; as we move into the twenty-first century, most Americans die in old age. Consider that in 1900, life expectancy was 47 years at birth, compared to 76 years for those born in 1991, an increase of fully twenty-eight years.

- In 1940 only about 30 percent of Americans lived to age 65; today 80 percent celebrate their 65th birthday, a fact that has enormous implications for government provisions of social security and Medicare.

- In 1900 persons who did reach their 65th birthday could expect to live nearly twelve more years. Today a 65 year old can expect to live more than seventeen additional years. This is the average life expectancy; many Americans will live twenty-five or thirty more years past age 65.

FIGURE 7–6

WIDENING GENDER GAP IN LIFE EXPECTANCY AT AGE 65

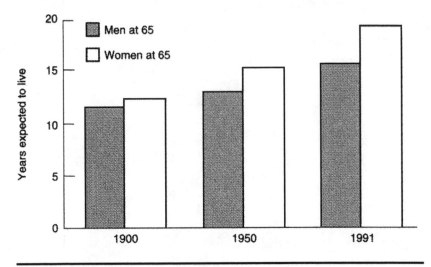

- There has been a widening gender gap in life expectancy. Throughout the twentieth century, women have had fewer children, and medical advances have meant that fewer die from childbirth complications. Women's life expectancy at age 65 currently exceeds men's by almost four years (19 versus 15 years).

- In 1994 there were 20 million women and 14 million men over age 65, a ratio of three to two.

- This growing femininization of the elderly population, along with the aging baby boomers, means that by the year 2010, almost half (48%) of all adult women (over age 21) in the nation will be at least 50 years old or older.

- There is little difference in the numbers of men and women in their forties and fifties; the gender gap comes with age.

FIGURE 7–7

CHANGES IN LIFE EXPECTANCY OVER TIME BENEFIT EVERYONE, BUT ESPECIALLY WOMEN AND WHITES

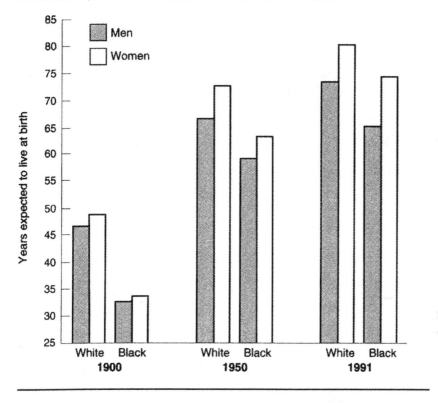

- Life expectancy at birth varies by both race and gender, with black men having the lowest life expectancy at birth (64.6 years compared to 72.9 years for white men) and white women the highest life expectancy from the day they are born (79.6 years compared to 73.8 years for black women). These life expectancies are stark testimony to the cumulation of advantage and disadvantage by race in American society.

- Differences in life expectancy by race and gender narrow as individuals reach their 65th birthday, with white women expected to live on average only two years longer than black women once they reach age 65 (19.2 years compared to 17.2 years) and white 65-year-old men expected to live only two years longer than black men of that age (15.4 years compared to 13.4 years).

FIGURE 7–8

RACE AND GENDER GAP IN LIFE EXPECTANCY NARROWS AS AMERICANS REACH AGE 65

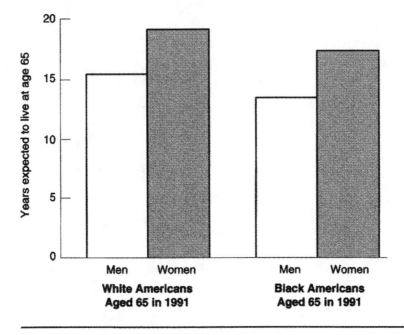

- In the 1980s there was an improvement in life expectancy for those reaching age 65, regardless of race and gender, with the biggest improvement (an increase of over one year) shown for white men.

- For the oldest old, there is a reduced race effect: black men and women who survive to age 85 are likely to live longer than their white counterparts.

- White women are the most likely to live to age 85, but black women who do reach 85 have more years of life expectancy. Similarly, black men who live to age 85 have a slightly higher life expectancy than do white men in their mid-80s.

FIGURE 7–9

CHRONIC ILLNESS IS MORE PREVALENT AS AMERICANS AGE

Top Five Chronic Conditions for Persons Aged 45 and Over, 1989

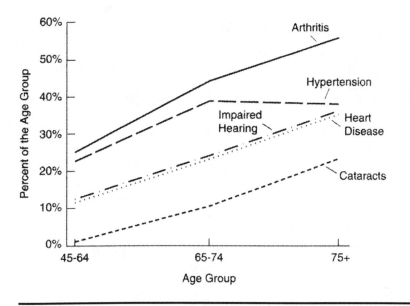

- Americans are living longer but not necessarily healthier. As more Americans live to be octogenarians, a rising number will experience a period of frailty, with mounting infirmity among the oldest old.

- An increased life span translates into increasing prevalence of chronic illnesses. For example, more than half of Americans aged 65 and older report having arthritis, and this condition is especially high among women and blacks (with almost two out of three older black women having arthritis).

- Americans have experienced major changes in the causes and timing of death. In 1900 the leading causes of death in the United States were infectious diseases, especially pneumonia and tuberculosis, often striking children and young adults; in the 1990s the leading causes of death are heart disease, cancer, and stroke, with death rates for these diseases increasing with age.

FIGURE 7–10

HEALTH STATUS DECLINES WITH AGE

Respondent-Assessed Health by Age Group, 1992

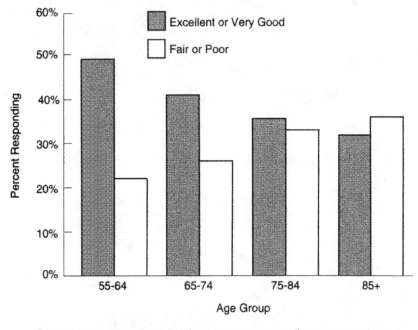

Respondents categorized their health status as excellent, very good, good, fair, or poor.

- Health status declines with age, but there remain significant numbers of healthy older Americans. Almost half (49%) of Americans aged 55–64 describe their health as excellent or very good, and almost a third (31.4%) of those 85 and older see themselves as healthy.

FIGURE 7-11

THE NEED FOR ASSISTANCE INCREASES WITH AGE

Persons Needing Assistance with Everyday Activities, 1990–1991

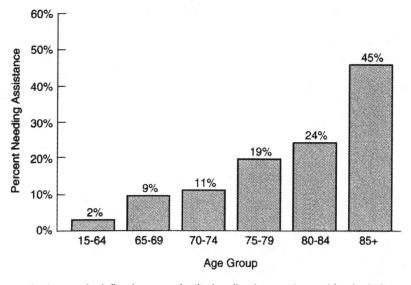

Assistance is defined as a noninstitutionalized person's need for the help of another person, because of a health condition which has lasted for at least three months. Everyday activities are defined as bathing, getting around inside the home, and preparing meals.

- As they age, increasing numbers of Americans require health care and assistance. About 7 million Americans over the age of 65 depend on others for help with activities of daily living.

- Almost half of those over age 85 who are not institutionalized have difficulty in performing activities of daily living.

- It is estimated that only 6% of Americans aged 65–74 have Alzheimer's disease but that as many as 50% of those 85 and older have some signs of the disease.

FIGURE 7–12

HEALTH AFFECTS ACTIVITY FOR OLDER BLACK AMERICANS MORE THAN FOR OLDER WHITE AMERICANS

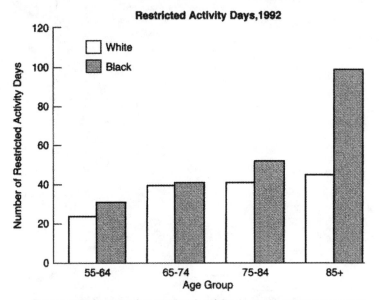

Data reported are number restricted-activity days per person per year as a result of acute and chronic conditions, by race and age group.

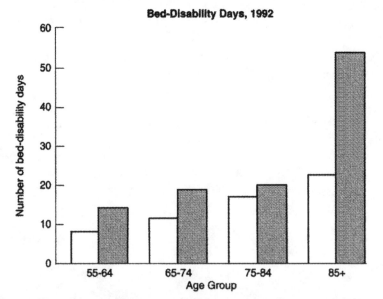

Data reported are numbers of bed-disability days per year as a result of acute and chronic conditions, by race and age group. Data are based on household interviews of the civilian noninstitutionalized population.

- With age, health problems are increasingly likely to limit activity, with older black Americans more likely to experience more days of restricted activity and bed disability than older white Americans (of those who are not institutionalized).

- Differences in health and activity level by race reflect the cumulation of advantage and disadvantage of those better or worse off economically throughout their life course.

FIGURE 7–13

NURSING HOME RESIDENCY IS INCREASING OVER TIME AND WITH AGE AND DIFFERS BY RACE

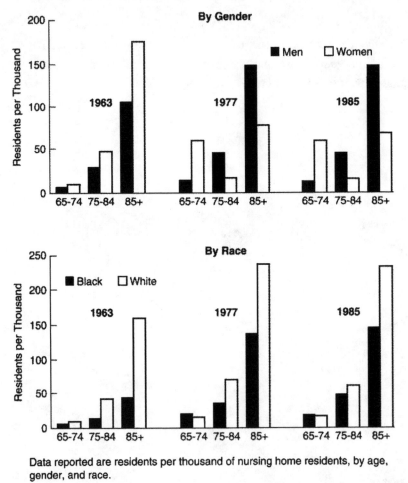

Data reported are residents per thousand of nursing home residents, by age, gender, and race.

- In 1990, about 1.8 million Americans were living in nursing homes.

- Older white Americans are more likely to be in a nursing home than are older black Americans.

- While only 1 percent of those aged 65–74 lived in a nursing home in 1990, nearly one in four of those aged 85 or older was in a nursing home.

FIGURE 7-14

GROWING NUMBERS OF AMERICANS IN THEIR 50s AND EARLY 60s HAVING AGING PARENTS

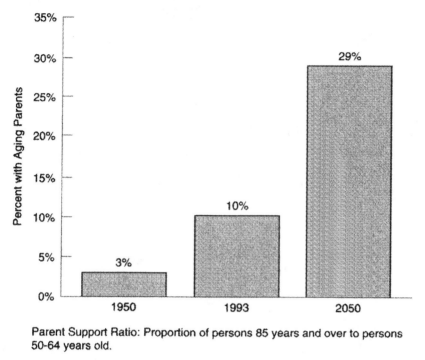

Parent Support Ratio: Proportion of persons 85 years and over to persons 50-64 years old.

- For many older people, family networks are an important social and economic resource; most older people rely on relatives for help when they need assistance with day-to-day activities of living. Americans are likely both to be caregivers and eventually to require caregiving as they age.

- It is estimated that in the coming century not only adults in midlife but also older Americans will be involved in more caregiving—of their yet older parents, aunts and uncles, spouses, siblings, and disabled children—as well as in providing child care to grandchildren and great-grandchildren.

- In 1990 3.2 million grandchildren (5% of all children) lived in homes maintained by their grandparents, and in 30% of the cases the children's parents did not live with them.

- Demographers construct a parent-support ratio of the proportion of persons 85 years old and older to those 50–64 years old who are likely to care for them. In 1950 there were only three of the oldest old for every 100 Americans in their prime adult years; by 1993 this had increased threefold and is anticipated to triple again over the next six decades.

- This changing ratio of adults to aging parents has important implications for families, but it also means fewer taxpayers supporting the financial and health care costs of older cohorts of Americans.

- A 1992 national survey of Americans found that almost one in three women and men aged 55 and over serve as informal caregivers of family, friends, or neighbors. Women, however, spend the most time providing care.

- It has been estimated that two out of three 50-year-old women have at least one living parent, compared to only one in three in 1940.

FIGURE 7–15

**OLDER WHITE WOMEN ARE ESPECIALLY SUSCEPTIBLE
TO HIP FRACTURES**

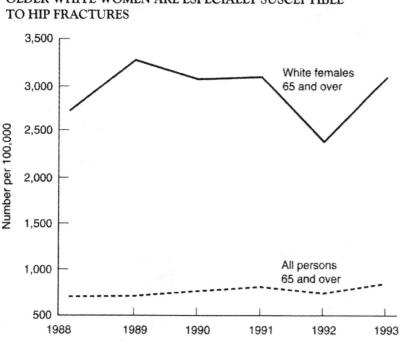

- Older people are prone to debilitating injury, requiring extensive care. For example, three out of every hundred white women aged 65 or older fractured a hip in 1993.

- Becoming injured or sick, or caring for an ailing or infirm spouse or relative, can be stressful and may curtail an older person's involvements with the outside world.

FIGURE 7–16

LIVING ALONE INCREASES WITH AGE, ESPECIALLY FOR WOMEN

Percentage of Americans Living Alone, by Age and Sex, 1993

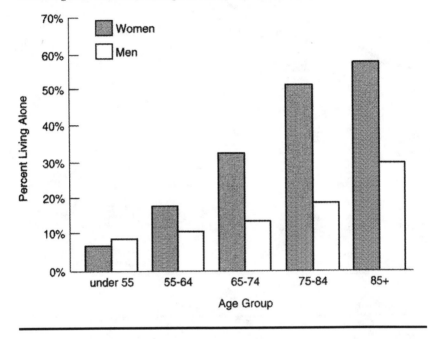

- Growing numbers of older Americans are at risk of social isolation.

- Older Americans are more likely than younger Americans to live alone. In 1990 9.2 million Americans aged 65 and older were living alone, a number expected to increase to 15.2 million by 2020.

- The proportion living alone increases with age, such that while only 25% of Americans aged 65–74 live alone, of those 85 and older, almost twice as many (47%) live alone.

- Women are more likely to live alone as they age, without the presence and potential support of a spouse, given the typical age disparity between husbands and wives, women's longer life expectancy, and the fact that older women are less likely to remarry than are older men. Half the women aged 75–84 live alone, compared to 18.4% of men in that age group. Of those 85 and older, 54% of women and 32.6% of men live alone. In contrast, only 14 percent of women and 10 percent of men in the 45–64 age range live alone.

• Living arrangements matter. Married elders are better off in terms of health and psychological and economic well-being than are those who are single, divorced, or widowed, and those living with others are similarly better off than those who live alone.

FIGURE 7–17

OLDER WHITE WOMEN ARE THE MOST LIKELY TO LIVE ALONE

Americans Living Alone, by Age, Race, and Sex, 1993

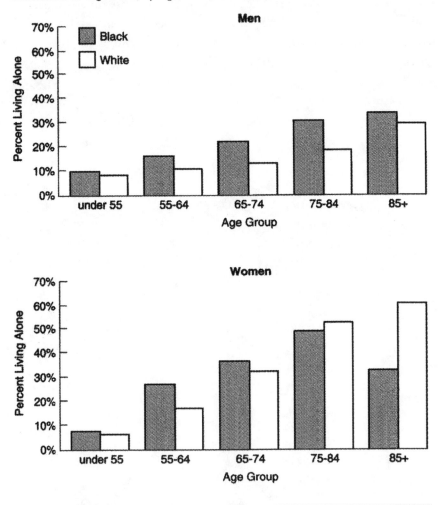

- In 1993 eight out of ten elderly who lived alone were women. Most likely to live alone are white women 85 years old or older.

- Longevity trends, along with increases in divorce, widowhood, and choices never to marry, mean that a growing number of Americans in the later years of adulthood will be single.

FIGURE 7–18

OLDER WHITE MEN HAVE HIGHER SUICIDE RATES
THAN THE REST OF THE POPULATION

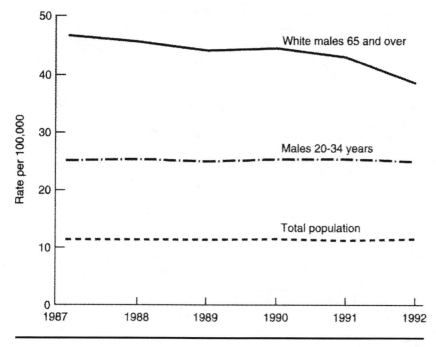

- One outcome of social isolation is suicide. Men are more likely to commit suicide than are women, with older white men the most vulnerable.

FIGURE 7–19

OLDER AMERICANS ARE INCREASINGLY LIKELY TO BE EDUCATED

Older Americans' Educational Achievement, 1947–1993

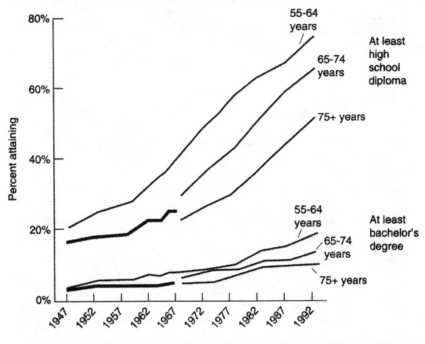

- Older Americans are not necessarily "old." We need a new life stage to describe the seasoned adults who may be in their 60s and 70s but are better educated and healthier than this age group has ever before been throughout history.

- In 1940, only 17% of those 55 and older had a high school diploma. By 1993 almost two in three (66%) of those aged 65–74 and 52% of those over 75 had at least a high school diploma.

- Almost eight in ten Americans aged 55–64 had at least a high school diploma in 1993 and almost one in five had a college degree. This means that the elderly of the future will be even better educated than is currently the case.

FIGURE 7-20

SIGNIFICANT PORTIONS OF OLDER AMERICANS
REPORT NO LIMITATIONS IN ABILITY
TO PERFORM PERSONAL OR ROUTINE CARE

Men and Women Without Limitation in Selected Activities, 1992

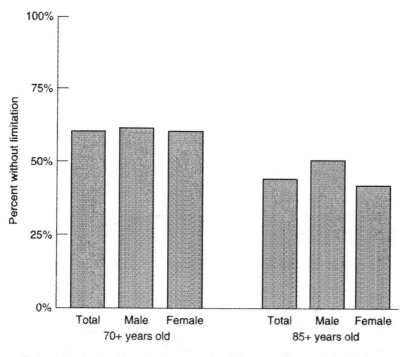

Data are based on household interviews of the civilian noninstitutionalized population. Personal and routine care includes activities such as eating, bathing, dressing, getting around the home, doing everyday household chores, doing necessary business, shopping, or getting around for other purposes.

- Medical advances and lifestyle changes have increased the numbers of Americans with no disabilities and few, if any, serious health problems.

- A majority of Americans aged 70 and older (60.3%) and significant proportions of those 85 and older (43.4%) report no limitations in their ability to perform routine activities, such as chores, shopping, and getting around for other purposes.

FIGURE 7–21

DRAMATIC DROP IN POVERTY OF OLDER AMERICANS OF ALL RACES

Persons 65 and Over Who Are in Poverty, 1959–1990

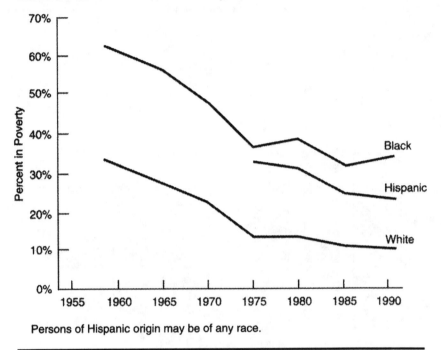

Persons of Hispanic origin may be of any race.

- Older Americans are, on average, better off economically than at any other time in the history of the nation, with social security, pensions, and personal assets (including savings) creating a "three-legged stool" of economic security.

- Both the amount and the coverage of public and private retirement benefits have increased over the past fifty years, with social security benefit increases from 1968 to 1972 and the establishment of automatic cost-of-living social security increases in 1975 dramatically improving the economic status of the elderly of all races.

- Social security income and supplemental security income (a means-tested benefit for the older or disabled) provide an income floor for the economically disadvantaged. This means that poor Americans may actually become more economically secure as they reach 65.

FIGURE 7–22

THE LIKELIHOOD OF ECONOMIC HARDSHIP INCREASES WITH AGE

Persons 65 Years and Over Who Are in Poverty or Near Poverty, 1989

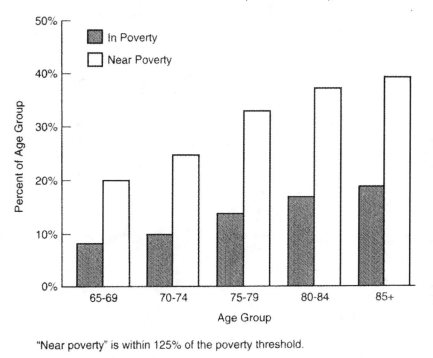

"Near poverty" is within 125% of the poverty threshold.

- The proportion of older persons (aged 65 and older) in poverty in 1960 was 35%; in 1970 it dropped 10 percentage points to 25%. By 1992 it had been cut in half to 13%. However, significant numbers of older Americans are poor, and a greater proportion of the elderly than the nonelderly are much more likely to have incomes just above the poverty level.

- Economic hardship increases with age, with 18% of Americans aged 85 and older living in poverty and an additional 27% near poverty. This could reflect both cohort differences (those moving into their mid-60s and 70s are better educated and have greater income and assets) and age differences (the oldest old, for example, are more likely to be widowed and therefore without their spouse's pensions).

FIGURE 7-23

**OLDER AMERICANS, AND ESPECIALLY BLACKS,
HAVE LESS INCOME AS THEY AGE**

Elderly households with yearly Income Less Than $10,000, 1989

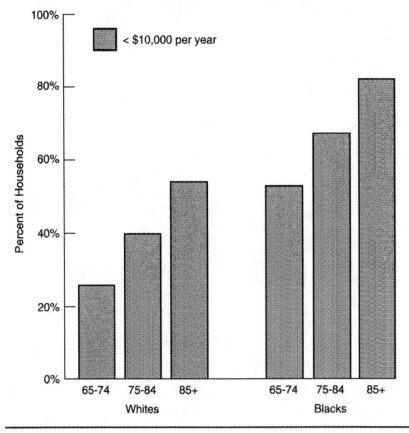

• Households headed by older black Americans are especially vulnerable to economic hardship, with African Americans less likely than other Americans to have pension benefits and savings.

• Older individuals who live alone, especially widows, are more likely to be below the poverty level than those living with others; over 60% of black women aged 65 and older who live alone are poor.

FIGURE 7-24

MANY AMERICANS ARE NOT PREPARED FINANCIALLY FOR RETIREMENT, 1995

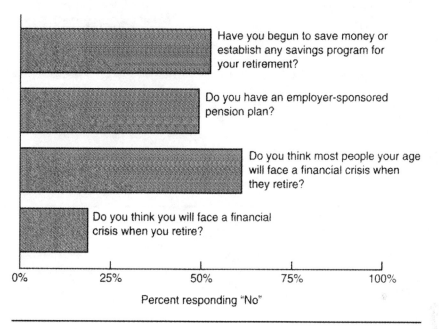

Have you begun to save money or establish any savings program for your retirement?

Do you have an employer-sponsored pension plan?

Do you think most people your age will face a financial crisis when they retire?

Do you think you will face a financial crisis when you retire?

0% 25% 50% 75% 100%

Percent responding "No"

- Future generations may not be as economically secure as current retirees as they move into their later years.

- About three in four Americans think most people their age will face a financial crisis when they retire.

- The downward mobility of the middle class, with rising debt, falling (or stagnant) income, and job insecurity, increasingly forms the backdrop in which retirement decisions are made.

FIGURE 7–25

OLDER AMERICANS WHO ARE BETTER OFF FINANCIALLY ARE THE MOST LIKELY TO HAVE INCOME FROM PENSIONS AND FROM EARNINGS

Percentage receiving:	Income Quintiles				
	Lowest income	2nd	3rd	4th	Highest income
Social Security	85%	96%	95%	95%	88%
Pensions	8	26	50	67	67
Earnings	5	9	19	29	46
Income from assets	31	56	75	87	96
Assistance	22	8	3	1	0

- A smaller percentage of future retirees may in fact have adequate pension coverage than is currently the case. Only 40% of American workers had employer-sponsored pension plans in 1990, with those employed in small, private firms the least likely to have such programs.

- The trend by employers toward a shift from defined-benefit plans (guaranteeing a set pension) to defined-contribution plans (placing funds in a savings account) may reduce the economic resources of those covered by such plans.

- Most older Americans have income from social security; those who are better off are likely to have income from pensions, earnings, or assets.

- Pension receipt expanded among African-American retirees in the 1970s and 1980s, in part reflecting the pensions provided to government employees.

FIGURE 7-26

A STEADY DECLINE IN THE EMPLOYMENT OF OLDER MEN

Labor Force Participation Rates of Men and Women 65 Years and Over,
1900–1993

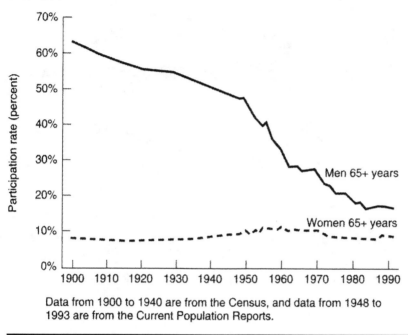

Data from 1900 to 1940 are from the Census, and data from 1948 to
1993 are from the Current Population Reports.

- Although many older Americans are healthy, educated, and sea-soned citizens, they are frequently sidelined from the mainstream of society. The nation offers few meaningful roles for this segment of the population.

- Older men are progressively leaving the labor force. As we entered the twentieth century, the majority (63%) of men aged 65 and older were active workers; by 1995 only about one in six (16%) older men were employed. By contrast, about the same proportion (8%) of women age 65 and older were employed at the beginning of the twentieth century as were working in 1995.

FIGURE 7–27

GENDER TRENDS IN EMPLOYMENT OF OLDER WORKERS ARE BEGINNING TO CONVERGE

Labor Force Participation Rates of Older Men and Women, 1948–1995

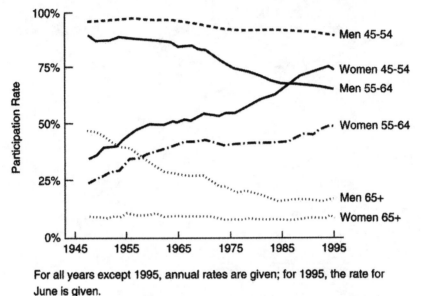

For all years except 1995, annual rates are given; for 1995, the rate for June is given.

- Even men in their 50s and 60s have been leaving the labor force; women in this age group, however, have been entering or remaining in the workforce. From 1950 to 1995 (for the 55–64 age group), male participation fell by 20% (from 86.9% to 66.5%), whereas female participation for this same age group rose by 20% (from 27% to 47.3%).

- Women in their 50s are more likely to be in the workforce than ever before in the history of the nation.

- Most retiring workers in the United States go from full-time, continuous employment to full-time, continuous leisure, with few alternative pathways (such as phased retirement in the form of part-time or part-year jobs) and little assistance in developing life plans for the next three decades (or more) of their lives.

- Over 5 million American workers aged 50–64 report that they would like to continue working longer if their employer offered to train them for a new position, their employer increased their position, or their employer offered to transfer them to a less stressful job or a job with shorter working hours.

• Employers are less likely to provide training to older, as opposed to younger, workers.

FIGURE 7–28

**A SMALL BUT SIGNIFICANT PROPORTION OF OLDER WORKERS
ARE LIKELY TO BE UNEMPLOYED**

Unemployment Rates by Age

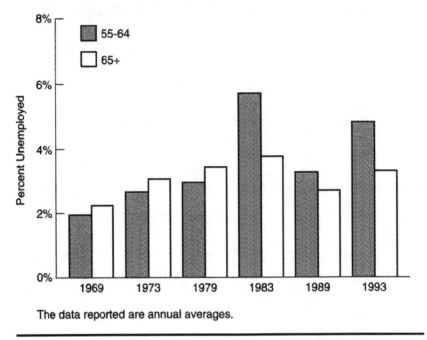

The data reported are annual averages.

- A small but significant proportion of older workers have been unemployed over the years.

- Older workers who are displaced are more likely than young unemployed persons to remain out of work longer and to drop out of the labor force if not rehired.

- Growing numbers of older Americans are encouraged to leave the labor force as companies restructure and downsize, and many expect to continue doing so in the future.

- It is estimated that 80% of the Fortune 100 corporations provided an early retirement incentive program at least once from 1979 through 1988. Such incentive packages offering pensions or lump-sum payments continue to be common in the 1990s.

FIGURE 7–29

ONE IN FOUR OLDER AMERICANS VOLUNTEERS FOR CHURCH, SYNAGOGUE, SCHOOLS, OR CIVIC ORGANIZATIONS

Persons 55 and Over Performing Unpaid Volunteer Work for Organizations, 1992

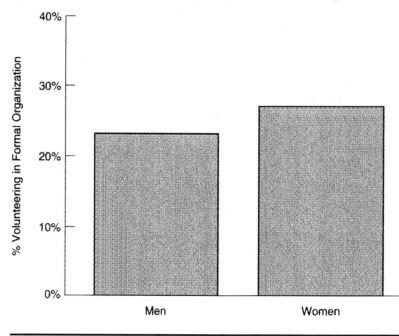

- Older Americans are almost as likely as younger Americans to volunteer for churches, schools, or civic organizations. Data from a 1992 nationwide survey reveal that more than one in four Americans over age 55 volunteers, with men and women about equally likely to do so. This represents 13.7 million older Americans actively serving as volunteers. Another 6 million say they are willing and able to volunteer.

- Almost half (47%) of the formal volunteering of older Americans is done through religious organizations; the other half involves service clubs and organizations, schools, hospitals, and senior citizen centers.

- More older Americans participate in informal volunteer activities (helping individuals) than engage in volunteer work for organizations. When volunteering is defined as "working in some way to help others for no monetary pay," a national survey found that 30% of those 55 and older help others by doing volunteer work on an informal basis.

- Unlike paid work, volunteer work does not decline with age. Almost one in four (23%) Americans aged 75 and older serves as a formal volunteer.

- The fact that systematic data on volunteer participation are not collected regularly points to the nation's focus on paid, as opposed to unpaid, work.

FIGURE 7–30

MEDICARE CONTINUES TO GROW

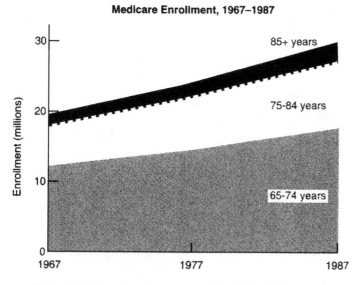

This graph is the plot of three years 1967, 1977, 1987.

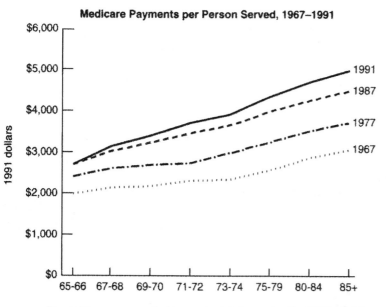

Payments were converted to constant dollars using the CPI for "all items."
Payments exclude amounts for HMO services.

• Shifts in the age distribution of the American population are having a major impact on the economy. Both government officials and citizens are beginning to ask what this will mean for the rest of the population.

• Medicare is a national health insurance program for older Americans, providing medical care for individuals 65 and older, regardless of income. Growing numbers of older Americans are enrolled in Medicare, and the costs rise with age.

FIGURE 7–31

**SOCIAL SECURITY PAYMENTS KEEP PACE
WITH INCREASING COSTS OF LIVING**

Monthly Payments for Social Security and AFDC, 1950–1993

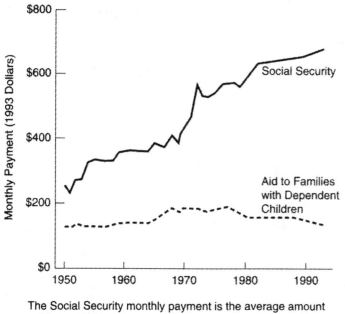

The Social Security monthly payment is the average amount
paid to retired workers.

- Social Security reflects a national commitment to providing a public pension to older workers. Most elderly Americans and their spouses are covered by this program.

- Social Security payments are adjusted to represent the changing costs of living, contributing to the economic security of older Americans and increasing expenditures on this program. In contrast, trends in Aid to Families with Dependent Children (AFDC) do not include cost-of-living increases.

- In addition to Social Security, older Americans who are poor or disabled can qualify for additional assistance in the form of Supplemental Security Income (SSI).

FIGURE 7–32

RISING COSTS OF BENEFITS FOR OLDER AMERICANS

Percent of Federal Budget spent on Social Security
and Medicare, 1936–1993

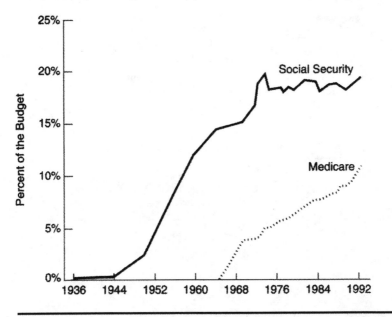

- The costs of benefits for elderly people (Medicare, Social Security) have mushroomed; they constitute over 30% of the federal budget.

- Medicare is projected to be one of the fastest-growing items in the federal budget, as a result of both increasing numbers of recipients and the rising costs of health care.

FIGURE 7-33

COSTS OF MEDICAID FOR OLDER RECIPIENTS ARE INCREASING

Average Medicaid Payments, 1972–1993

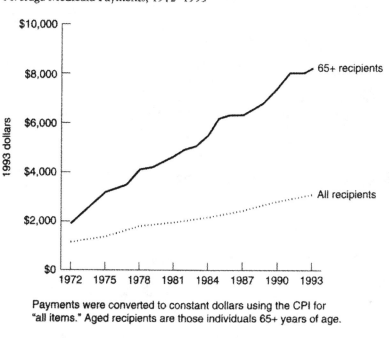

Payments were converted to constant dollars using the CPI for
"all items." Aged recipients are those individuals 65+ years of age.

- Medicaid has been a safety net for very frail and infirm older Americans, paying for about half (52%) the costs of long-term (nursing home) care.

- Although the absolute number of Americans aged 65 and older on Medicaid has not increased since the 1970s, the cost of Medicaid for older recipients (frequently for long-term care) has increased.

- Older Americans and people with disabilities account for only 27% of Medicaid recipients, but fifty-nine cents of every Medicaid dollar is spent on these groups. (Contrary to popular opinion, most Medicaid dollars do not go to women and children on AFDC.)

- Many middle-class older Americans who require nursing home care "spend down" (deliberately exhaust) their savings to qualify for Medicaid.

- The number of people requiring nursing home care is currently 1.5 million and is expected to rise to between 4 and 5 million over the next thirty years.

FIGURE 7–34

MOST AMERICANS REPORT THAT THEY DO NOT WANT TO BALANCE THE FEDERAL BUDGET AT THE COST OF MEDICARE OR SOCIAL SECURITY, 1995

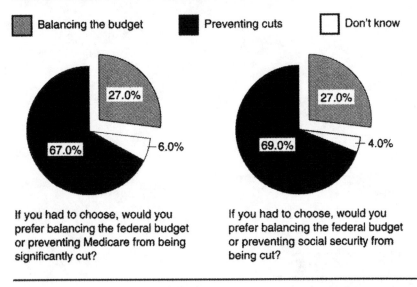

■ Balancing the budget   ■ Preventing cuts   □ Don't know

27.0% 67.0% 6.0%

27.0% 69.0% 4.0%

If you had to choose, would you prefer balancing the federal budget or preventing Medicare from being significantly cut?

If you had to choose, would you prefer balancing the federal budget or preventing social security from being cut?

- A recent survey (N.Y. Times/CBS Poll, September 1995) found that most Americans, regardless of their political affiliation, would prefer to preserve Medicare and Social Security.

- Changes in the age distribution of the nation, along with rising medical costs, suggest that the current system, with its emphasis on dependency, may require substantial revision, especially as there will be progressively fewer prime-age adults to foot the bills.

LOOKING TO THE FUTURE

In contemplating aging, most Americans are likely to look backward, not forward. For example, surveys have shown that many Americans equate old age with retirement or reaching age 65. But the information presented in this chapter suggests that prevailing stereotypes about growing older generally and about older people in particular are out of step with reality.

Most Americans also link aging with decline and dependency, yet growing numbers of older adults are healthy, vigorous, independent individuals who will live twenty, twenty-five, or even thirty or more years beyond retirement. With the exception of economic security, the nation has focused more on helping the dependent rather than fostering independence in old age.

The realities of an aging society and the costs of equating aging with dependence are already being reflected in the growing costs to employers of providing pensions and health insurance to current retirees and the burgeoning costs to the nation of government benefits to the elderly. This public safety net—of Social Security, Medicare, and Medicaid—has been successful in reducing economic deprivation and in providing for the health care of older Americans. But as we look to the future, these programs are in trouble (Figure 7–35).

Lee Iacocca, in assuming leadership of the Chrysler Corporation, is reported to have said to a gathering of autoworkers in Detroit: "If you don't know a retired Chrysler worker, get to know one. Each of you is working to support a retiree." Iacocca's observation is increasingly relevant for the nation, as there are growing numbers of retirees in proportion to employees in the workforce. The ratio of workers covered by Social Security to those receiving social security retirement benefits was over sixteen to one in 1950; by 2030 it is expected to fall to two to one. This means that there will be only two workers in the labor force for every one retiree.

Two trends in particular will have enormous impact for both this and coming generations: the revolution in health and longevity and the revolution in retirement timing. Americans are living healthier longer and are retiring at progressively earlier ages. In combination with the aging

FIGURE 7–35

ASSETS OF THE PUBLIC SAFETY NET ARE FALLING

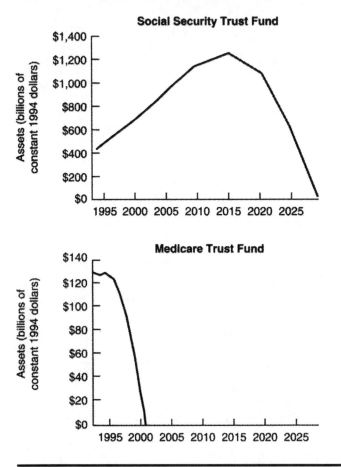

of the baby boom cohort, these trends are producing growing numbers of vital, capable individuals in the postretirement years. It has been estimated that 2 million people retire each year, a number that will expand to 3 million per year by the year 2000. In January 1996, the first members of the post–World War II baby boom generation celebrated their fiftieth birthday. How can we invent new roles for this emerging wave of "young" workers soon to retire from their career jobs?

Retirement is, in fact, a relatively recent phenomenon. In earlier

FIGURE 7–36

NUMBER OF WORKERS SUPPORTING RETIREES IS DECLINING DRAMATICALLY

Number of Workers per Person receiving Social Security, 1950–2030

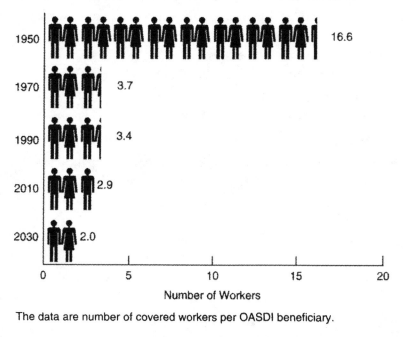

The data are number of covered workers per OASDI beneficiary.

times and in other places, children as well as old people have been expected to be productive members of society. Today social forces structure childhood as a time of preparation and learning; these same forces all converge to render many individuals in the later years of adulthood marginal to the broader community. The reality is that the nation provides few opportunities for active, meaningful involvement for older Americans. Yet a large body of research evidence suggests that purpose and meaning contribute to quality of life in terms of health, vigor, and psychological well-being.

Earlier chapters have documented that our society is structured around and sustained by gainful employment. Paid work is the pathway to economic independence for Americans in the prime of adulthood.

But employment represents more than income. Jobs provide a framework for organizing and integrating social existence—not only individual lives but also the various institutions, organizations, and activities of the broader community. Consider how the rhythm of traffic and the scheduling of television reflect the workday. For most adults, paid work is a major, if not the principal, source of purposive activity, social relations, independence, identity, and self-respect. Holding a job is the way that most Americans become integrated and acknowledged as adult members of the larger community. But our notions of paid work and workers on the one hand, and the growing numbers of able, older Americans, on the other, are at cross purposes. For example.

- Corporations increasingly are downsizing, laying off, or inducing the early retirement of large numbers of older workers, even those in their 50s.
- Despite laws prohibiting age discrimination, few employers are willing to hire or retrain people over age 50.
- Pension policies and incentive packages effectively encourage early retirement.
- Social Security rules discourage postretirement employment, yet significant numbers of older Americans are capable of and want to continue working.
- Large numbers of Americans of all ages engage in unpaid volunteer work, but such activity does not provide the status, identity, and structure that society allocates to paid jobs in the economy.

These are examples of structural lag, a situation whereby norms, policies, and practices fail to keep pace with the demographic realities and possibilities of an aging society. They also illustrate a key challenge: to develop new institutional arrangements that promote the social integration and productivity of older adults. Just as we have seen the social construction of adolescence as a way-station from childhood to adulthood during the first half of this century, so now there is emerging a way-station from midlife to old age. We call this way-station—considering its current amorphous shape and for want of a better word—*limbo.*

What can be said about the social value, as well as the lives, lifestyles, and prospects, of individuals who may be healthy, skilled, and energetic but who are retired from their career jobs? If you are not working, you are not, by definition of most Americans, being productive. If you are not working, you are without the status and identity associated with holding a position in the occupational structure. If you are not working, your life lacks the structure and order provided by the time demands and deadlines of a job. If you are not working, you lack the community and camaraderie of coworkers. If you are not working and physically able, even wanting to do so, you are in limbo.

There is another group in limbo as well: older workers who are effectively "retired" from meaningful work, though they continue on the job. The first half of life is considered the optimal time to be trained and retrained, with little training occurring after age 50. Retirement today increasingly reflects a glass curtain of limited prospects for meaningful activity, training, or advancement for workers over 50 and a glass exit sign in the form of exit incentive packages that push workers out of the labor force years before they had anticipated retiring. The "normal" retirement age of 65 is rapidly becoming a cultural relic, as growing numbers of workers leave the labor force in their 50s and 60s and a small group resolves never to retire.

Psychologist Erik Erikson describes mature adulthood as vital involvement in generative activities, in other words, active participation in meaningful roles. The institutionalization of retirement as a universal status passage has effectively deprived most older Americans of opportunities for paid employment. And the absence of purposive, institutionalized roles for older Americans severely limits opportunities for social integration and productive activity.

Two important forms of continued productive engagement for those in their 50s, 60s, and 70s (and beyond) are paid employment, part or full time, and unpaid volunteer work. While it is true that retired individuals are able to find opportunities for volunteer work, the fact is that the structure of society and the economy is ordered around full-time jobs and full-time workers, as are organizations, families, and communities. The concept of job is equated with paid work. And the concept of worker applies largely to those in young adulthood through midlife.

What institutional arrangements can be invented, recombined, or reinvented to foster competence and productivity in the later years of adulthood? Competence represents the skills, abilities, beliefs, values, and commitments required to meet life's challenges. Clearly productivity requires competence, but it also requires opportunity. The assignment of the productive work of society to those in early and middle adulthood affects not only opportunities for productive work in later adulthood but also older adults' sense of their own capability and usefulness.

In the twenty-first century we are likely to see the prevailing view of retirement itself retired, unlinking age and retirement. There are, of course, existing practices that already separate retirement from age. For example, military personnel who retire after twenty or thirty years of service frequently begin second careers. And professional athletes typically retire while still in their late 20s or 30s, then go on to other roles. At the other end of the continuum, politicians and judges often "age in place," with only severe illness or death moving them out of work. Competency-based employment is also a way of separating age from retirement, with ability rather than age determining continued employment. What is required is an institutional environment and public- and private-sector policies that remove the disincentives to work and increase the options for productive activity at all ages.

Traditionally employment and retirement have been seen as antithetical, with individuals moving inevitably and irreversibly from one to the other as they age. But there is an emerging blurring of boundaries between work and retirement and, indeed, a trend toward the engagement of a more temporary, contingent workforce at every life stage. A growing form of postretirement productive activity is the practice of contract work, with organizations offering and individuals taking on jobs (either paid or unpaid) for an agreed-on period of time or performance output. One variation of contract work is the corporate job bank, where firms use their own (or community) retirees as temporary workers to staff positions during vacation periods or leaves of absence. A second option is partial retirement, permitting older workers to reduce their hours on the job gradually. Still another possibility is the second or even third or fourth career, with individuals leaving one job for another more consistent with their abilities or interests, at times starting their own businesses. A permutation is that individuals volunteer their time and talents, not in their spare time but as jobs in service to their communities, sometimes launching new programs addressing identified needs. A fourth strategy, the corporate retiree volunteer program, is a way for organizations to use their retirees for community service and for retirees to preserve an attachment to their coworkers and places of work. As the sociologist Shinkap Han points out, work is as much about people and their relations as it is about tasks. Corporate retiree volunteer programs enable retirees to maintain relationships that were fostered on the job.

The way we foster dependency rather than independence in old age is costly in terms of the quality of life older Americans experience; it is also costly to the whole of the nation as it struggles to provide economic security and health care to its burgeoning older population. In looking at older people, Americans have focused on their needs rather than their abilities. Removing barriers to independence and fostering opportunities for social involvement and productive activity can both improve the quality of life for older Americans and help to prevent or ameliorate the impairments conventionally associated with growing older. As an untapped community resource, this group of seasoned citizens has much to offer to society, and especially to the next generation of Americans.

One can envision socially constructive alternatives, where workers cut back on their work hours, move to less demanding jobs, start new careers, or take on work assignments with fixed time limits (in the way that consultants and construction workers typically do). Similarly, volunteer and community service could be better recognized as legitimate work, with volunteer participation regarded and encouraged in the same way as labor force participation and measured as a basic function and output of our economic system. Retirees can be a potent force for social change, becoming a voluntary workforce helping to break the cycles of disadvantage experienced by many young Americans as they move through childhood and into adulthood, cycles that are so vividly described in earlier chapters of this book.

Americans may come to equate retirement and the later years of adulthood not with pure leisure but with a time of expanding options to engage in various types of meaningful and productive activity. The challenge is to identify the social forces and structures that shape avenues of opportunity that promote or, conversely, inhibit productive role involvements throughout adulthood.

8

CONCLUSION

A t the core of contemporary American concerns are two sets of problems, both threatening consequences of the first importance, and the two combined posing one of the more formidable challenges in the nation's history.

One set of problems is economic, involving a slowdown in the rate of economic growth, falling real wages for those at the lower end of the wage scale, rising inequality, and a fading belief in the American dream, particularly among the least advantaged members of society. Among those least advantaged are children living in poverty, whose numbers swell as family incomes at the bottom fall and the percentage raised by single parents rises. But social scientists have no widely accepted and precisely specified theories of why wages of the least skilled have been falling or why the rate of economic growth has slowed in recent decades. Their list of possible remedies accordingly reduces to a handful of policy proposals which, if adopted, should do "some good" to make a bad situation better: improved training and education should help raise the wages of the least skilled; higher saving, more investment, increased capital formation, and larger expenditures on research and development should help to raise the rate of economic growth.

The one certainty seems to be that no major government initiatives are likely to be launched under any of the headings just noted as long as the dominant priority in Washington is to reduce the federal deficit. Nor is there any reason to believe that natural forces will remedy those major economic ills the government seems destined to neglect. Market mechanisms as yet unforeseen may admittedly revive economic growth and reverse the fall in the wages of the least skilled. But to rely on that possibility is to concede that this nation's major economic difficulties can only be solved by accident, instead of by design.

The second set of problems at the core of present-day American concerns is more difficult to characterize. Falling wages and lagging growth are well-defined phenomena; a "decline in values" is not. But the vagueness of the problem in no way undermines the urgency of the concern. Something is terribly wrong, many are coming to believe. And what is perceived as a growing threat is variously characterized as "the unraveling of the moral fabric" of the country, or parents "doing battle with powerful trends in American culture." A seismic shift seems under way in the beliefs and values in this country, particularly those endorsed by the nation's youth. Not all of the associated changes have been for the worse, as many would hasten to point out. Since World War II, for example, the changing attitudes in society toward women and minorities have facilitated dramatic improvements in the access of these groups to better education and a wider range of occupational possibilities. But if tolerance in many quarters has been on the rise, allegiance to other values commonly judged as "good" seems in decline, including honesty, a sense of personal responsibility, respect for others anchored in a sense of the dignity and worth of every individual, and a willingness to give a helping hand to those who have suffered misfortune through no fault of their own. Something has gone awry, many now argue, in a society in which more and more teenagers are becoming unwed mothers, in which teenagers murder teenagers with impunity, in which civility, community, and safety are fast disappearing in many urban centers.

Here, too, as was true of undesirable economic trends, the causes are poorly understood. We know surprisingly little about the process whereby allegiance to ethical norms is transmitted from one generation to another. Much is made, for example, of the need to "teach values" in the nation's schools, as the influence of family and church in many children's lives seems to be diminishing, and the values learned on the street and from the media appear, to many, to leave much to be desired. What few have thought to ask is whether schools are equal to the task. To teach *about* values is relatively easy. To inculcate values is a far more demanding challenge. With the transmission process so poorly understood—and with the competition for allegiance to other norms so powerfully and pervasively peddled to the nation's youth by the media and its peers—how can schools be expected to become a major institution, or *the* major institution, for inculcating values in the nation's youth?

At the core of this second set of concerns is nothing less than a transformation of America's culture by forces not well understood, in directions many of its people do not want. If, at bottom, that is the problem, any solution of any note must be wide-ranging, persistent, and the product, if not of all of the people all of the time, then of most of the people much of the time. Will American society be equal to such a challenge? The associated national debate at present seems to be overshadowed by exchanges between warring factions offering simplicity of analysis and certainty of diagnosis in pursuit of the quick fix. There is no certainty. There are no quick fixes. And yet something must be done. Because as psychologist Erich Fromm reminds us:

> The history of man is a graveyard of great cultures that came to catastrophic ends because of their incapacity for planned, rational, voluntary reaction to challenge.

Sources for Figures

Chapter 1. Youth: Changing Beliefs and Behaviors

Figure 1–1 *Monitoring the future* (Survey Research Center, 1976–1992), a yearly survey of high school students conducted since 1976. The data in this, and following figures using these data, include only high school seniors, who have been interviewed every year.

Figure 1–2 U.S. Department of Commerce. Bureau of the Census. (1994). *Current population reports, Series P-20: Voting and registration in the election of November, 1992*, no. 466. Washington, DC: U.S. Government Printing Office.

Figure 1–3 Bars 1–3: Schab, F. (1991). Schooling without learning: Thirty years of cheating in high school. *Adolescence, 26*, 839–847. Bars 4–5: McCabe, D. L., & Bowers, W. J. (1994). Academic dishonesty among males in college: A thirty year perspective. *Journal of College Student Development, 35*, 5–35.

Figures 1–4 through 1–15 Survey Research Center. (1975–1992). *Monitoring the future*. Ann Arbor, MI: University of Michigan, Interuniversity Consortium for Political and Social Research. The figures are based on statistical analyses by the chapter authors.

Figures 1–16 and 1–17 Bastian, L. (1995). *Criminal victimization 1993*. Washington, DC: U.S. Department of Justice, Bureau of Justice Statistics.

Figure 1–18 Bar 1: Centers for Disease Control. (1991). Weapon-carrying among high school students—United States, 1990. *Morbidity and Mortality Weekly Report, 40*, 681–684. Bar 2: Centers for Disease Control. (1994). Health-risk behaviors among persons aged 12–21 years—United States, 1992. *Morbidity and Mortality Weekly Report, 43*, 231–235. Bar 3: U. S. Department of Justice. (1991). *Teenage victims: A National Crime Survey report*. Washington, DC: Bureau of Justice Statistics.

Bar 4: Louis Harris and Associates. (1994). *The American teacher, 1993: Violence in America's public schools.* New York: Louis Harris and Associates. Bars 5–6: Louis Harris and Associates. (1995). *The American teacher, 1994: Violence in America's public schools: The family perspective.* New York: Louis Harris and Associates.

Figure 1–19   Huizinga, D., Loeber, R., & Thornberry, T. (1993). Longitudinal study of delinquency, drug use, sexual activity, and pregnancy among children and youth in three cities. *Public Health Reports, 108,* 90–96.

Figure 1–20   Bars 1–2: Survey of California Lawyers. (1994, November). *California Bar Journal,* pp. 1, 4. Bars 3–5: Anderson, R. E., & Obershain, S. S. (1994). Cheating by students: Findings, reflections, and remedies. *Academic Medicine, 5,* 323–332.

Chapter 2: Crime and Punishment

Figure 2–1   U.S. Department of Justice. (1960–1995). *Crime in the United States (Uniform Crime Reports).* Washington, DC: Federal Bureau of Investigation.

Figure 2–2   World Health Organization. (1981–1993). *World health statistics annual.* New York: United Nations.

Figure 2–3   Bars 1, 3, 4: MacKellar, F. L., & Yanagishita, M. (1995). *Homicide in the U.S. Who's at risk?* Washington, DC: Population Research Bureau. Bar 2: National Center for Health Statistics. Centers for Disease Control. (1993). *Health United States, 1992.* Washington, DC: U.S. Government Printing Office.

Figure 2–4   U.S. Department of Justice. Federal Bureau of Investigation. (1994). *Crime in the United States, 1993.* Washington, DC: U.S. Government Printing Office.

Figure 2–5   Bar 1: Snell, T. (1993). *Correctional populations in the U.S., 1992.* Washington, DC: U.S. Government Printing Office. Bar 2: Canadian Centre for Social Statistics. (1992). *Adults' correctional services in Canada.* Ottawa: Minister of Supply and Services. Bars 3 and 4: Council of Europe. (1992). *Prison information bulletin.* Strasbourg: Council of Europe. Bar 5: Shikita, M., & Tsuchiya, S. (eds.), (1992). *Crime and criminal policy in Japan.* New York: Springer-Verlag.

Figure 2–6   Langan, P. A. (1988). *Historical statistics on prisoners in state and federal institutions, yearend 1925–86.* Washington, DC: U.S. Government Printing Office; Cahalan, M. W. (1986). *Historical corrections statistics in the United States, 1850–1984.* Washington, DC: U.S. Department of Justice, Bureau of Justice Statistics; Gilliard, D. K., & Beck, A. J. (1994). *Prisoners in 1993.* Washington, DC: U.S. Department of Justice, Bureau of Justice Statistics; Beck, A. J., & Gilliard, D. K. (1995). *Prisoners in 1994.* Washington, DC: U.S. Department of Justice, Bureau of Justice Statistics; Perkins, C. A., Stephan, J. J., & Beck, A. J. (1994). *Jails and jail inmates 1993–1994.* Washington, DC: U.S. Department of Justice, Bureau of Justice Statistics; U.S. Department of Justice, (1995, December 4). Press release.

Figure 2–7   Beck, A. J., & Gilliard, D. K. (1995). *Prisoners in 1994.* Washington, DC: U.S. Department of Justice, Bureau of Justice Statistics.

Figure 2–8   Council of Economic Advisors. (1994–1995). *Annual report to the president*. Washington, DC: U.S. Government Printing Office.

Figure 2–9   (A) Freeman, R. B. (1991). *Crime and the employment of disadvantaged youths*. Cambridge, MA: National Bureau of Economic Research. (B) Beck, A. J., & Shipley, B. E. (1989). *Recidivism of prisoners released in 1983*. Washington, DC: U.S. Department of Justice, Bureau of Justice Statistics.

Figure 2–10   U.S. Department of Justice. (1992). *Justice expenditure and employment, 1990*. Washington, DC: Bureau of Justice Statistics.

Figure 2–11   U.S. Department of Commerce. (1965–1992). *State government finances*. Washington, DC: U.S. Government Printing Office.

Figure 2–12   Author's projection from Uniform Crime Reports (1983–1993) and U.S. Bureau of the Census (1995).

Chapter 3. Economic Developments

Figure 3–1   *Business Week*. (1995, March 13). Harris Poll.

Figure 3–2   Bureau of Economic Analysis. (1955–1992, March). *Survey of current business, monthly business statistics*. Washington, DC: U.S. Government Printing Office. Output is defined as GNP in constant 1987 dollars. Man-hours are total, seasonally adjusted hours of wage and salary, nonagriculture, private-sector, and government workers.

Figure 3–3   (A) Council of Economic Advisors. (1985, 1994, 1995) *Economic Report of the President*. Washington, DC: U.S. Government Printing Office. (B) Council of Economic Advisors. (1995). *Economic Report of the President*. Tables B45, B47. Hourly earnings are defined as "real, average hourly earnings of total private, nonagricultural industries" and are converted to constant 1982 dollars using the consumer price index (CPI) for urban wage earners and clerical workers. Hourly compensation is defined as "real compensation per hour for the nonfarm business sector." It includes wages and salaries of employees plus employers' contributions for social insurance and private benefit plans, plus an estimate of the wages, salaries, and supplemental payments for the self-employed. Current-dollar hourly compensation figures are converted to constant 1982 dollars using the CPI for all urban consumers. Data for 1994 are preliminary.

Figure 3–4   Bureau of the Census. (1992). *Current population reports*, Series P-60. Wahington, DC: U.S. Government Printing Office, Bureau of the Census. (19xx). *Historical statistics of the U.S., Colonial times to 1970*, Washington, DC: U.S. Government Printing Office.

Figure 3–5   Bureau of the Census, (1976). *The statistical history of the United States, Colonial times to 1970*. Washington, DC: U.S. Government Printing Office. Bureau of the Census. (1992). *Money income of households, families, and persons in the United States: 1992*. Washington, DC: U.S. Government Printing Office. Current dollar figures were converted to constant 1992 dollars using the Consumer Price Index-Urban Consumers (CPI-U-X1). Average annual rates are based on annual compounding between the two end-point years.

Figure 3–6   Council of Economic Advisors. (1995). *Economic report of the president, 1995.* Washington, DC: U.S. Government Printing Office. Data were prepared by the Bureau of Labor Statistics using the Current Population Survey. All wages are in constant 1982–1984 CPI-U-X1 dollars. Each percentile's wage is defined similarly to the following example for the tenth percentile wage: ranking all wage earners from lowest wage to highest wage, the tenth percentile wage is the highest wage among the lowest 10% of wage earners. The median percentile is the highest wage among the lowest 50% of all wage earners.

Figure 3–7   AFDC data: U.S. Administration for Children and Families. (1975–1992). Quarterly public assistance statistics. Food stamps data: Department of Agriculture (1979–1992). Annual historical review of FNS programs. Department of Agriculture. *Characteristics of food stamp households, September 1976 and September 1978.* Washington, DC: U.S. Government Printing Office. Current dollar figures are converted to constant 1992 dollars using the CPI-U-X1. Because food stamp payments do not depend on the sex of family members, the food stamp figures are the average payments for all three-member families.

Figure 3–8   Bureau of the Census. (1992). *Poverty in the United States: 1992.* Washington, DC: U.S. Government Printing Office. Bureau of the Census. (1994, December). *How we're changing: Demographic state of the nation.* Washington, DC: U.S. Government Printing Office

Figure 3–9   Bureau of the Census. (1984, 1987, 1990, 1994). *Statistical abstract of the United States.* Washington, DC: U.S. Government Printing Office.

Figure 3–10   Rose, S. J. (1993, November–December). Declining family incomes in the 1980s: New evidence from longitudinal data. *Challenge.* Income quintiles stratified by ten-year income average; data from the Panel Study on Income Dynamics of the Survey Research Center, University of Michigan.

Figure 3–11   National Center for Education Statistics. (1994). *Dropout rates in the United States.* Washington, DC: Department of Education.

Figure 3–12   Barton, P., & LaPointe, A. (1995). *Indicators of performance in higher education.* Princeton, NJ: Educational Testing Services.

Figure 3–13   Manski, C. F. (1992–1993, Winter). Income and Higher Education. *Focus, 14* (3), 18. College enrollee figures are for 18- and 19-year-old high school graduates during the period 1975–1984 and are taken from the annual October Current Population Survey (U.S. Bureau of the Census). College graduate figures are taken from the "High School and Beyond Survey" (U.S. Department of Education, NCES, 1986) and are based on the college graduation rate for the high school class of 1980.

Figure 3–14   Bound, J., and Johnson, G. (1992, June). Changes in the structure of wages in the 1980s: An evaluation of alternative explanations. *American Economic Review, 82,* 371–392. Entry-level wages are defined as wages of individuals with an average of five years' work experience. Using Current Population Survey (CPS) (March release) data, Bound and Johnson calculated the 1973, 1979 and 1988 figures by (1) splitting the CPS data into subsamples, in our case, individuals with zero to nine years' work experience (hence, a mean of five years), (2) regressing the wages on work experience using dummy variables for educational attainment (i.e., less than high school, high school, college degree), and then (3) calculating mean wages and mean work experience Bound and Johnson assumed that individuals with only a high school degree start work at the age of 16 and that college degree holders began work at 22 years of age.

Figure 3–15   Bureau of the Census. (1974–1990). *Money and income of households and persons in the U.S.* (Washington, DC: U.S. Government Printing Office. Ratios are based on relative median income of each group, adjusted to constant 1990 dollars using the CPI-U-X1. "Non–high school" is based on the median income of individuals who did not complete at least one year of high school; "high school" income is based on the median income of all persons who have completed four years of high school; "college" income is base on the median income of all persons who completed four or more years of college.

Figure 3–16   Organization of Economic Cooperation and Development (OECD). Statistics Directorate. (1994). *Labour force statistics, 1972–1992.* Paris: Organization for Economic Cooperation and Development. OECD. (1994) *OECD Economic Outlook 1994.* Rates are defined as "unemployment rates: commonly used definition."

Figure 3–17   Office of Management and Budget. (1995). *Budget of the United States Government, Historical Tables.* Washington, DC: U.S. Government Printing Office.

Figure 3–18   Bureau of the Census. (1980, 1994). *Statistical Abstract of the U.S., 1980, 1994.* Washington, DC: U.S. Government Printing Office, 1991 AFDC figure is an unweighted average of 1990 and 1992 figures. All 1975 current dollar figures were converted to 1991 constant dollars using the CPI-U-X1.

Figure 3–19   Council of Economic Advisors. (1995). *Economic report of the president, 1995.* Washington, DC: U.S. Government Printing Office.

Figure 3–20   Council of Economic Advisors. (1995). *Economic report of the president, 1995.* Washington, DC: U.S. Government Printing Office.

Figure 3–21   Council of Economic Advisors. (1995). *Economic report of the president, 1995.* Washington, DC: U.S. Government Printing Office.

Chapter 4:

Figure 4–1   Hobbs, F. (1990). *Child's well-being: An international comparison.* Washington, DC: U.S. Department of Commerce, Bureau of the Census.

Figure 4–2.   Department for Economic and Social Information and Policy Analysis. (1994) *Demographic yearbook: 1992*. New York: United Nations.

Figure 4–3   National Center for Health Statistics. (1960–1994). *Vital statistics of the United States, 1960–1990*. Vol. 1: *Natality*. Washington, DC: Public Health Service.

National Center for Health Statistics. (1964–1994). *Vital statistics of the United States, 1960–1990*. Vol. 3: *Marriage and divorce*. Washington, DC: Public Health Service.

Figure 4–4   National Center for Health Statistics. (1974–1994). *Vital statistics of the United States, 1970–1990*, Vol. 3: *Marriage and divorce*. Washington, DC: Public Health Service.

Figure 4–5   U.S. Bureau of the Census. (1960–1995). *Marital status and living arrangements, 1959–1994*. Washington, DC: U.S. Government Printing Office.

Figure 4–6   U.S. Bureau of the Census. (1970–1995). *Marital status and living arrangements, 1969–1994*. Washington, DC: U.S. Government Printing Office.

Figure 4–7   U.S. Bureau of the Census. (1996). Unpublished 1994 data tables.

Figure 4–8   Analysis using data from the National Longitudinal Survey of Youth (NLSY).

Figure 4–9   National Center for Health Statistics. (1960–1995), (1995). Vital Statistics of the United States, 1960–1991, Vol. 1: Natality. Washington, D.C.: Public Health Service.

National Center for Health Statistics. (1994–1995). *Advance report of final natality statistics, 1992–1993*. Hyattsville, MD: National Center for Health Statistics.

Figure 4–10   Analysis using data from the NLSY.

Figure 4–11   Analysis using data from the NLSY.

Figure 4–12   U.S. Bureau of the Census (1996). Unpublished 1994 data tables.

Figure 4–13   Bureau of Labor Statistics. (1950–1976). Unpublished reports and data tables.

Bureau of Labor Statistics. (1977–1989). Handbook of Labor Statistics. Washington, D.C.: U.S. Department of Labor. Bureau of Labor Statistics. (1996). Unpublished reports and data tables.

Figure 4–14   U.S. Bureau of Labor Statistics. Unpublished data tables.

Figure 4–15   U.S. Bureau of Labor Statistics (1996). Unpublished data tables.

Figure 4–16   Casper, L. (1995). *Current population reports, Household economic studies: What does it cost to mind our preschoolers?* Washington, DC: U.S. Department of Commerce, Bureau of the Census.

Figure 4–17   Luster, T., and Small, S.A. (1990, May). *Youth at risk for teenage par-*

enthood. Paper presented at the Creating Caring Communities Conference, East Lansing, MI.

Department for Economic and Social Information and Policy Analysis. (1995). *Demographic yearbook: 1992.* New York: United Nations.

Figure 4–18   Analysis using data from the NLSY.

Figure 4–19   Analysis using data from the NLSY.

Figure 4–20   National Center for Health Statistics (1974–1994). *Vital Statistics of the United States, 1969–1990.* Vol. 1: *Natality.* Washington, DC: Public Health Service.

National Center for Health Statistics. (1995). *Advance report of final natality statistics, 1993.* Hyattsville, MD: Public Health Service.

Figure 4–21   National Center for Health Statistics (1959–1995). *Vital Statistics of the United States, 1959–1991.* Vol. 1: *Natality.* Washington, DC: Public Health Service.

National Center for Health Statistics. (1994–1995). *Advance report of final natality statistics, 1992–1993.* Hyattsville, MD: Public Health Service.

Figure 4–22   National Center for Health Statistics (1974–1995). *Vital Statistics of the United States, 1969–1991.* Vol. 1: *Natality.* Washington, DC: Public Health Service.

National Center for Health Statistics. (1994–1995). *Advance report of final natality statistics, 1992–1993.* Hyattsville, MD: Public Health Service.

Figure 4–23   U.S. Bureau of the Census (1996). Unpublished 1994 data tables.

Figure 4–24   Analysis using data from the NLSY.

Figure 4–25   Analysis using data from the NLSY.

Figure 4–26   Analysis using data from the NLSY.

Figure 4–27   Analysis using data from the NLSY.

Figure 4–28   Analysis using data from the NLSY.

Figure 4–29   Analysis using data from the NLSY.

Chapter 5

Figure 5–1   Rainwater, L. (1992). Why the U.S. antipoverty system doesn't work very well. *Challenge,* Jan/Feb, pp. 30–35.

Figure 5–2   Rainwater, L. and Smeeding, T. (1995). U.S. doing poorly compared with others. New York: National Center for Children in Poverty, Columbia University, School of Public Health.

Figure 5–3   U.S. Bureau of the Census. (1961–1996). *Current population reports: Consumer income, series P-60.* Washington, DC: U.S. Government Printing Office.

Figure 5–4   U.S. Bureau of the Census. (1961–1996). *Current population reports: Consumer income, series P-60.* Washington, DC: U.S. Government Printing Office.

Figure 5–5   U.S. Bureau of the Census. (1996). Unpublished data tables.

Figure 5–6   U.S. Bureau of the Census. (1961–1996). *Current population reports: Consumer income, series P-60.* Washington, DC: U.S. Government Printing Office.

Figure 5–7   U.S. Bureau of the Census. (1974–1996). *Current population reports: Consumer income, series P-60.* Washington, DC: U.S. Government Printing Office.

Figure 5–8   U.S. Bureau of the Census. (1962–1994). *Statistical abstract of the United States.* Washington, DC: U.S. Government Printing Office.

Figure 5–9   Children's Defense Fund. (1992). *The state of America's children.* Washington, DC: Children's Defense Fund.

Figure 5–10   U.S. Bureau of the Census. (1996). Unpublished data tables.

Figure 5–11   National Center for Children in Poverty. (1993). *Young children in poverty.* New York: Columbia University School of Public Health.

Figure 5–12   Children's Defense Fund. (1992). *The state of America's children.* Washington, DC: Children's Defense Fund.

Figure 5–13   U.S. Bureau of the Census. (1996). Unpublished data tables.

Figure 5–14   U.S. Bureau of the Census. (1961–1993). *Current population reports: Consumer income: Poverty in the United States, series P-60 1959–1992.* Washington, DC: U.S. Government Printing Office.

Figure 5–15   U.S. Bureau of the Census. (1961–1996). *Current population reports: Consumer income, series P-60.* Washington, DC: U.S. Government Printing Office.

Figure 5–16   U.S. Bureau of the Census. (1961–1996). *Current population reports: Consumer income: Poverty in the United States, series P-60.* Washington, DC: U.S. Government Printing Office.

Figure 5–17   Analysis using data from the NLSY.

Figure 5–18   U.S. Bureau of the Census. (1996). Unpublished data tables.

Figure 5–19   Analysis using data from the NLSY.

Figure 5–20   U.S. Bureau of the Census. (1961–1996). *Current population reports: Consumer income, series P-60.* Washington, DC: U.S. Government Printing Office.

Figure 5–21   U.S. Bureau of the Census (1996). Unpublished data tables.

Chapter 6

Figure 6–1   Grissmer, D.W., Kirby, S.N., Berends, M., & Williamson, S. (1994). *Student achievement and the changing American family.* Rand Institute on Education and Training. Santa Monica, CA: Rand Corp.

Figure 6–2   Grissmer, D.W., Kirby, S.N., Berends, M., & Williamson, S. (1994). *Student achievement and the changing American family.* Rand Institute on Education and Training. Santa Monica, CA: Rand Corp.

Figure 6–3   Grissmer, D.W., Kirby, S.N., Berends, M., & Williamson, S. (1994). *Student achievement and the changing American family.* Rand Institute on Education and Training. Santa Monica, CA: Rand Corp.

Figure 6–4   Grissmer, D.W., Kirby, S.N., Berends, M., & Williamson, S. (1994). *Student achievement and the changing American family.* Rand Institute on Education and Training. Santa Monica, CA: Rand Corp.

Figure 6–5   Grissmer, D.W., Kirby, S.N., Berends, M., & Williamson, S. (1994). *Student achievement and the changing American family.* Rand Institute on Education and Training. Santa Monica, CA: Rand Corp.

Figure 6–6 through Figure 6–8   Robitaille, D.F., & Garden, R.A. (1989). *The IEA Study of mathematics II: Contexts and outcomes of school mathematics.* New York: Pergamon.

Figure 6–9   Stevenson, H., & Stigler, J. (1987). *The learning gap: Why our schools are failing and what we can learn from Japanese and Chinese education.* New York: Summitt Books.

Figure 6–10   Kirsch, I. (1993). *Adult literacy in America.* Princeton, NJ: Educational Testing Service.

Figure 6–11   Barton, P., & Lapointe, A. (1995). *Indicators of performance in higher education.* Princeton, NJ: Educational Testing Service.

Chapter 7

Figure 7–1   U.S. Bureau of the Census. (1994). *Current population reports, series P-25.* Nos. 98, 310, 519, 917, 1018, 1045.

U.S. Department of Commerce. *Statistical Abstract of the United States.* Washington, DC: U.S. Government Printing Office.

Figure 7–2   U.S. Bureau of the Census. (1994). *Current population reports, series P-25.* Nos. 98, 310, 519, 917, 1018, 1045.

U.S. Department of Commerce. *Statistical Abstract of the United States.* Washington, DC: U.S. Government Printing Office.

Figure 7–3   U.S. Bureau of the Census. (1994). *Current population reports, series P-25.* Nos. 98, 310, 519, 917, 1018, 1045.

U.S. Department of Commerce. *Statistical Abstract of the United States.* Washington, DC: U.S. Government Printing Office.

Figure 7–4   U.S. Bureau of Labor Statistics. (1992). *Outlook 1990–2005.* Washington, DC: U.S. Government Printing Office.

Figures 7–5   National Center for Health Statistics. (1995) *Health United States, 1994.* Hyattsville, MD: Public Health Service.

Figure 7–6   National Center for Health Statistics. (1995) *Health United States, 1994.* Hyattsville, MD: Public Health Service.

Figure 7–7   National Center for Health Statistics. (1995) *Health United States, 1994.* Hyattsville, MD: Public Health Service.

Figure 7–8   National Center for Health Statistics. (1995) *Health United States, 1994.* Hyattsville, MD: Public Health Service.

Figure 7–9   National Center for Health Statistics. (1990). Current estimates from the National Health Interview Survey, 1989. *Vital and Health Statistics,* ser. 10, no. 176.

U.S. Senate Special Committee on Aging, American Association of Retired Persons, Federal Council on Aging, and the U.S. Administration on Aging. (1991). *Aging America: Trends and projections.* Washington, DC.

Figure 7–10   National Center for Health Statistics. (1995). *Health United States, 1994.* Hyattsville, MD: Public Health Service. Table 1.

Figure 7–11   U.S. Bureau of the Census. (1992). *Sixty-five in the United States.* Current Population Reports. Washington, DC: Government Printing Office. Figure 3–6.

U.S. Bureau of the Census. (1990). *Current population reports, P70–19, The need for personal assistance with everyday activities: Recipients and caregivers.* Washington, DC: U.S. Government Printing Office. Table B.

Figure 7–12   National Center for Health Statistics. (1995). *Health United States, 1994.* Hyattsville, MD: Public Health Service. Tables 4, 5

Figure 7–13   National Center for Health Statistics. (1995). *Health United States, 1994.* Hyattsville, MD. Public Health Service. Table 1.

Figure 7–14   U.S. Bureau of the Census. (1995, May). *Statistical brief, sixty-five in the United States.* SB/95–8. Washington, DC: Government Printing Office.

Figure 7–15   National Center for Health Statistics, Centers for Disease Control and Prevention, (1993).

Figure 7–16   Saluter, A. F. (1994). *U.S. Bureau of the Census, marital status and living arrangements.* Current Population Reports, Series P20–478. Washington, DC: U.S. Government Printing Office. Table 7.

Figure 7–17   Saluter, A. F. (1994). *U.S. Bureau of the Census, marital status and living arrangements.* Current Population Reports, Series P20–478. Washington, DC: U.S. Government Printing Office. Table 7.

Figure 7–18   National Center for Health Statistics (1987–1992).

Figure 7–19   U.S. Bureau of the Census. (1994). *Current population reports, series P20, 45, 77, 99, 121, 138, 158, 169, 182, 274, 356, 415, 451, 476.* Washington, DC: U.S. Government Printing Office.

Figure 7–20   National Center for Health Statistics. (1995). *Health United States, 1994.* Hyattsville, MD: Public Health Service. Table 3.

Figure 7–21   U.S. Bureau of the Census. (1992). *Sixty-five in the United States.* Current Population Reports. Washington, DC: U.S. Government Printing Office. Figure 4–4.

Littman, M. (1991). *U.S. Bureau of the Census. Poverty in the United States: 1990.* Current Population Reports, Series P-60, no. 175. Washington, DC: U.S. Government Printing Office.

Figure 7–22   U.S. Bureau of the Census. (1992). *Sixty-five in the United States.* Current Population Reports. Washington, DC: U.S. Government Printing Office. Figure 4–4.

Radner, D. B. (1991). Changes in the incomes of age groups, 1984–1989. *Social Security Bulletin, 54* (12), Table 8.

Figure 7–23   U.S. Congress. House Select Committee on Aging. (1992). *Elderly Households, a profile.* Report No. 102–912. 102d Congress, 2nd Session, 1992.

U.S. Bureau of the Census. (1995) *The 1989 American Housing Survey.* Data on CD-ROM.

Figure 7–24   *New York Times.* (1995, March 26).

Figure 7–25   Grad, S. (1992). *Income of the population 55 and over, 1990.* U.S. Department of Health and Human Services, Social Security Administration. Washington, DC: U.S. Government Printing Office.

Figure 7–26   U.S. Bureau of Labor Statistics. (1988). *Labor force statistics derived from the current population survey, 1948–87.* Washington, DC: U.S. Government Printing Office.

U.S. Bureau of the Census. (1975). *Historical statistics of the United States, colonial times to 1970.* Bicentennial ed. pt. 1. Washington, DC: U.S. Government Printing Office.

Figure 7–27   U.S. Bureau of Labor Statistics. (1996). Unpublished data.

Figure 7–28   U.S. Department of Labor. (1994). *Report on the American workforce.* Washington, DC: U.S. Government Printing Office. Table 1.10.

Figure 7–29   U.S. Bureau of Labor Statistics. (1990). *Thirty-eight million persons do volunteer work.* Press release. USDL, 90–145.

Figure 7–30   (A) Darnay, Arsen, J. (ed.). (1994). *Statistical record of older Americans.* Detroit, MI: Gale Research.

U.S. Bureau of Data Management and Strategy. Health Care Financing Administration. (1996). Unpublished data.

(B) National Center for Health Statistics. (1994). *Health United States, 1993.* Hyattsville, MD: Public Health Service. Table 148.

Figure 7–31   Social Security Administration. (1994). *Annual statistical supplement to the Social Security Bulletin*. Washington, DC: U.S. Government Printing Office. Table 3.C4.

Figure 7–32   Social Security Administration. (1994). *Annual statistical supplement to the Social Security Bulletin*. Washington, DC: U.S. Government Printing Office. Tables 4.A1, 8.A1.

U.S. Bureau of the Census. (1994). *Statistical abstracts of the United States*. Washington, DC: U.S. Government Printing Office. Table 504.

Figure 7–33   U.S. Department of Health and Human Services. Social Security Administration. (1993). *Annual statistical supplement, 1992 to the Social Security Bulletin*. Washington, DC: U.S. Government Printing Office.

U.S. Department of Health and Human Services. Social Security Administration. (1994). *Annual statistical supplement, 1994 to the Social Security Bulletin*. Washington, DC: Government Printing Office.

Figure 7–34   Clymer, A. (1995, October 26). Americans reject big Medicare cuts, a new poll finds. *New York Times/CBS News Poll*, pp. A1, D23–24.

Figure 7–35   Board of Trustees. (1994). *Federal Old-Age and Survivors Insurance and Disability Insurance Trust Funds, annual report, 1994*. Washington, DC: U.S. Government Printing Office Federal Hospital Insurance Trust Fund. Board of Trustees. (1994). *Annual report, 1994*. Washington, DC: U.S. Government Printing Office.

Figure 7–36   Federal Old-Age and Survivors Insurance and Disability Trust Funds. Board of Trustees. (1995). *Annual report*. Washington, DC: U.S. Government Printing Office.

Notes

Preface

1. Bronfenbrenner (1975).
2. Bronfenbrenner (1969).
3. Bronfenbrenner (1975).

Chapter 1

1. The data for figure 1.1 are derived from *Monitoring the future* (Survey Research Center, 1976–1992), a yearly survey of high school students that has been conducted since 1976. The data in this, and following figures, includes over 280,000 high school seniors, who have been interviewed every year. All figures using these data are based on new calculations by the authors of this chapter, except for Figure 1–5.
2. See Hardaway, Marler, and Chaves (1993). Although well-respected polls show that today's adults report almost the same frequency of religious attendance that adults reported in the 1950s, data on actual church attendance do not bear this out.
3. See Schab (1991).
4. Survey Research Center, University of Michigan, Press release, December, 1994.
5. Survey Research Center, University of Michigan, Press release, December, 1994.
6. Louis Harris and Associates (1994; 1995).
7. See Bastian (1993). Data are from the National Crime Victimization Survey.
8. See Snyder & Sickmund (1995). This report summarizes and interprets 20 years of juvenile crime and incarceration data.
9. See Anderson & Obershain (1994).

Chapter 2

1. See National Center for Health Statistics (1994) for cause of death statistics by age and racial groups.
2. The homicide death rates were compiled from United Nations (1993); MacKellar & Yanagishita (1995); U.S. Department of Justice, (1960–1994); and National Center for Health Statistics, (1993).
3. See Snyder and Sickmund (1995).
4. See Blumstein (1995); Dembo, Hughes, Jackson, & Mieczkowski (1993).
5. U.S. Department of Justice press release, December 4, 1995.
6. See Beck and Greenfeld (1995).
7. Incarceration data and rates for 1995 are from National Institute of Justice press release of December 3, 1995. Incarceration rates for 1920, 1950, and 1980 were calculated by the author.
8. See Piehl (1994).
9. See Fagan (1993); Dembo, Hughes, Jackson & Mieczkowski (1993).
10. See Piehl (1994).
11. Figures calculated by author from U.S. Department of Commerce (1965–1992).
12. U.S. Department of Justice (1995b).
13. See Walinsky (1995).
14. U.S. Department of Commerce (1965–1992).
15. Center on Juvenile and Criminal Justice (1995).
16. U.S. Department of Justice (1995b).
17. U.S. Department of Justice (1995b).
18. Author's projection from Uniform Crime Reports (1983–1993) and U.S. Bureau of the Census, *Population Projections*.
19. Costs were estimated by Klaus (1994), based on self-reported economic losses reported to the National Crime Victimization Survey. These include losses due to theft, damage, hospitalization, and missed work days. Costs resulting from homicides are not included.
20. *New York Times*, August 19, 1995.

Chapter 3

1. "Productivity" here is defined as output per manhour, the same measure used in Figure 3–2.
2. The two most fashionable measures of total output for any economy are gross national product (GNP) and gross domestic product (GDP). For any given year, the first estimates the total production of goods and services using inputs supplied by U.S. residents. The second (GDP) estimates the total production of goods and services within the United States. The two measures differ in focus: GNP estimating what U.S. citizens produce (whether at home or abroad) and GDP estimating production within the confines of the United States (irrespective of the citizenship of the producers).

3. To identify the growth of GNP over time requires that the total production figure for each year be corrected for inflation (or in economists' jargon, that actual or "nominal" values be corrected to "real" values). If, say, the recorded value of GNP is $1 trillion in 1970 and $4 trillion in 1990, one cannot infer that total output quadrupled in 20 years, because much of the recorded increase of $3 trillion may have been caused by prices rising rather than output expanding. In subsequent figures, then, such phrases as "GNP in constant 1987 dollars" simply mean that all estimates (in this case, of GNP) have been adjusted for inflation by expressing all totals in the prices of a given year (in this case, the year 1987).

4. Some analysts discount this slowdown by noting that the rates of growth recorded in the 1950s and 1960s were abnormally high compared with the average growth recorded by the American economy since the mid-nineteenth century. Although empirically correct—the immediate postwar performance was exceptional—most economists remain deeply troubled by the extent of the subsequent slowdown, primarily because that slowdown has brought in its wake the kinds of problems outlined in this chapter. From a long-run perspective, productivity growth since 1973 has been the worst twenty-year performance since the Civil War. Other conventional measures of overall economic performance (not graphed) also indicate a significant slowdown, including GNP (or GDP) per capita, output per worker (rather than output per man hour plotted above), and output per unit of input (the last of these including inputs other than labor, such as capital equipment and natural resources). Estimates of these alternative measures can be found in Stein & Foss (1995, pp. 7, 13, 53).

5. "Constant 1982 dollars" on the vertical axis of Figure 3–3A indicates that all wages have been expressed in terms of the price level prevailing in 1982. The choice of which correction to use to convert actual wages to constant dollar terms is largely dictated by the availability of price indexes.

6. Some analysts put a brighter face on these wage trends by emphasizing that a shorter work week reflects more leisure, and some of the rise in fringe benefits has gone to finance vacations, sick leaves, and the like. How much the reduction of the work week has been voluntary and how much involuntary is impossible to say. The relative importance of paid time off in the rapid rise of fringe benefits is suggested by the following. Between 1953 and 1993, the proportion of payroll devoted to health benefits rose by a multiple of 4.7 (from 3% of payroll to 14%), to retirement and saving benefits rose by a multiple of 2.6 (from 5% of payroll to 13%), and to payment for time not worked rose by less than half (from 7.5% of payroll to 11%).

7. The average measure used is the median (not the mean). The merits of the former are perhaps most easily explained by an example. If all students in a given high school are placed in a line, from the tallest to the shortest, the median height would be the height of the student in the middle; that is, that individual with an equal number of taller and shorter students standing on either side. One merit of the median as a measure of the average is that it is unaffected by

the occurrence of extreme cases at either end of the distribution. In the case of our line of students, for example, if a seven-foot male were added at one end and a midget at the other, the median height would remain unchanged.

8. How minor this boost is can be seen from the following example. If $12,000 is shared among 3.01 persons (the average household size in 1973), income per person is roughly $4,000. If two decades later the same $12,000 is divided among 2.63 persons (the average household size in 1993), the share of each rises to $4,563, or by 14% in twenty years. To correct the second bar in Figure 3–4B for a rise of this magnitude would leave unscathed the main message of that illustration, which is the markedly inferior growth record of the second period.

9. Roughly speaking, inflation-adjusted per capita personal income expresses— on a per person basis—the sum of all income-related receipts and disbursements (corrected for inflation), such as wages, rents, interest, profits, and government transfers less taxes.

10. Zinsmeister (1995, p. 45).

11. For those unfamiliar with the measure, a word of explanation is in order concerning the meaning of percentiles. Imagine 100 workers arranged in a line, from the lowest paid to the highest. The wage of the tenth percentile is roughly the wage received by the worker standing tenth from that end of the line which begins with the worker paid the least. (More rigorously, the tenth percentile wage is the highest wage among the lowest 10% of wage earners.) At this juncture, the careful reader may wonder why the family income of the highest income quintile can grow at rates (almost 1% a year) that exceed by quite a margin the growth rate of the ninetieth percentile of wage earners. The answer, in part, is that wages comprise only part of family income, and nonwage income—such as profits, dividends, rent, interest, and capital gains—tends to be a relatively more important income source for wealthy families.

12. The official U.S. poverty standard was established in the 1960s. Beginning with estimates of minimally adequate food budgets for families of different sizes, the poverty line was established for each family size by multiplying the dollar value of each food estimate by three. The controlling assumption was (and still is) that food typically represents about one-third of total family expenditure, particularly for families at the lower end of the income spectrum. The official poverty line, in reality, is therefore a set of lines—an array of dollar amounts that vary by family size. Those families whose incomes fall below the threshold for their family type are officially classified as poor. Income for purposes of this calculation includes money income (before taxes) but excludes noncash benefits received, such as food stamps and Medicaid.

Not surprisingly, this measure of poverty has been repeatedly assailed as inadequate. Those who argue that it overstates those in poverty usually focus on benefits not counted as income, such as food stamps and subsidized housing and health care. Those who argue that it understates poverty usually focus on factors that make disposable family income lower than pretax income, such as taxes, child-care costs, and medical expenses not covered by the government. One recent and controversial attempt to correct for these and other defects was made in response to a congressional request by a panel of experts at the National Academy of Sciences. Their revised measure, published in May 1995, suggested that the "official" count, once corrected in the manner they advocated, would give a poverty rate 1% to 3% higher than the present measure (including fewer poor on welfare but a larger number of working poor).

13. A growing concentration of wealth is suggested by the recent estimates of Edward Wolff. The "marketable wealth" he estimates held by "the richest one percent of wealth holders in the U.S." increased from 19.9% in 1976 to 35.7% in 1989 (the last year for which data are available) (1995).

14. Analysis is limited to "prime-age adults": those who begin each decade between the ages of 22 and 48 and thus end each decade between the ages of 32 and 58.

15. The data on college graduation are more problematic, because colleges do not keep track of students who enter but then transfer elsewhere.

16. For a recent survey on this puzzle, see Burtless (1995).

17. A similar propensity for running persistent annual deficits has not been evident among state governments. Indeed, state and local governments combined recorded a net surplus in every year from the late 1960s to the early 1990s. In a number of cases, this is not surprising. Thirty-nine states require the legislature to pass a balanced budget, and thirty-one require that the governor sign a balanced budget into law. In 1994, however, state and local governments collectively ran a deficit.

18. One reduction in federal spending that has been much smaller than originally anticipated is that associated with defense. The "peace dividend" accompanying the end of the cold war has been relatively modest, with the current military budget (roughly $250 billion) still as close to 85% of the average annual (inflation-adjusted) defense spending for the cold war years.

19. Devising comparable saving rates for different countries is an extremely complicated task, and for that reason, a graph depicting international comparisons is not included. One set of estimates by a recognized American authority for the period 1990–1992 suggests the relative magnitudes involved: the "average household saving rate" for the United States was about 60% of the average of four European nations—Germany, Britain, France, and Italy—and only about half that of Japan (Bosworth, 1995).

20. In terms of causal linkages developed early—but now applied to the global economy—by the mid-1990s, real or inflation-adjusted interest rates were historically high, suggesting a worldwide imbalance between desired investment and the supply of savings.

21. In 1970, as a percentage of GDP, the United States, West Germany, and Japan all spent about 1.8% on nondefense research and development. In 1991, the percentages spent were 1.9, 2.7, and 3.0, respectively (Karier, 1995).

22. Government funding for research and development is often viewed as one

form of public (versus private) investment, the other two being spending on physical infrastructure (such as roads and bridges) and on "human capital programs" to improve education and skills of the sort discussed previously. Whether each of these yields large or small returns for dollars spent is a topic of debate. But what would seem incontestable is that, given its preoccupation with deficit reduction, the federal government is unlikely to engage in large increased spending under any of these headings for the remainder of this century.

23. Some analysts have suggested that the recent surge in productivity in America (or in some measures of productivity) is indicative of a shift toward higher long-run growth rates. Skeptics are quick to point out that gains in productivity normally accompany recoveries from recession, and the short-run gains have no clear implications for the long run. The basic difficulty is our limited understanding of the process. As recently noted in one of the world's most respected economic periodicals, "if they are honest, economists admit that they know next to nothing about the underlying causes of productivity growth" (*The Economist*, Sept. 16, 1995, p. 18).

Chapter 4

1. We cite the rate of first marriage rather than the overall marriage rate because the latter is also influenced by the rate of divorce.
2. U.S. Bureau of the Census (1960–1995).
3. In this analysis, socioeconomic background was assessed primarily on the basis of the income of the family in which the future mother had grown up. In subsequent analyses, we shall also take into account other factors—such as the parents' education.
4. Note, however, that in all three ethnic groups the difference between women raised in near-poor versus poor families is consistently smaller than that between near-poor and middle-class backgrounds, a phenomenon that we examine in the next chapter.
5. Ventura (1995).
6. The contrast for Hispanic families is even smaller—from $10,400 to $23,000—a range of $12,000, with a mean of $18,000, higher than that for black families, but much lower than the average income for whites with young children ($35,600).
7. When first reported, these were defined as mothers who had never married, and to permit comparability we report the labor force participation rates for this same group from 1949 to 1994. Information on rates for divorced and for separated mothers is presented in the figures that follow.
8. Casper (1995).
9. Dryfoos (1990); National Research Council (1987).
10. Although, as we have seen, the percentage of cases in which fathers are given custody is growing, they are still in the minority. As a result, the higher proba-

bility associated with paternal custody may also have to do with the grounds on which custody was given to the father.

11. Analysis of data for women growing up under different forms of single-parent-hood revealed a pattern similar that shown in Fig 4–11. Most likely to become unmarried teenage mothers were the daughters of unmarried mothers, with children of divorce next in line, with the differences being maximized for women who had grown up in poverty. One reason that daughters from di-vorced families are at lower risk is that such families tend to have higher in-comes (see Figure 4–12).

12. Hispanics are omitted because breakdowns of birth rates by marital status for this ethnic group have only recently become available.

Chapter 5

1. U.S. Bureau of the Census (1992, p. A-7). In this series, see the following sec-tion on sources.

2. U.S. Bureau of the Census (1992, p. A-7).

3. Rainwater (1992).

4. These data come from the Luxembourg Income Study (Rainwater, 1992), the most extensive and respected ongoing investigation in this field. The figures pertain to the late 1980s or early 1990s. Since then, the poverty rate in the United States has been rising. For example, the poverty rate for all children under 18 in 1995 was 21.9. For this and other reasons documented later in this chapter, the rank order of the United States in this international comparison (and others to follow) is not likely to have changed appreciably in the past 10 years.
   For half of these countries, the data are from the early 1990s, for the rest, from the late 1980s.

5. Rainwater & Smeeding (1995b, p. 19).

6. By 1994, the poverty threshold for a two-parent family with two children living below the poverty line was a total income from all sources of no more than $15,029. The corresponding cutoff for a single-parent family with one child was $10,214. For this purpose, children are defined as all persons under 18 years of age.

7. Implications of this dual development for the future are discussed in Chapter 7.

8. Comparable data for this group were not previously available.

9. Woodrow (1992).

10. See U.S. Bureau of the Census (1993).

11. The statement disregards the comparatively small percentage of children living in single-father families.

12. For a description of sample and measures used from the NLSY, see appendix at the end of Chapter 4.

13. The graph is based on the latest published data available. They appear in the U.S. Bureau of the Census (1992).

14. It is of interest that the results for Hispanic young adults fell in between—closer to whites growing up in middle-class or near-poor households but approaching the same high risks as blacks for Hispanic youth raised in poverty.

15. Regrettably, no comparable data are available for other ethnic minorities—among them, Asians, Native Americans, and newly arrived immigrants from around the world.

Chapter 6

1. McMillen, Kaufman, and Whitener (1994); General Accounting Office (1990).
2. Stevenson and Stigler (1992).
3. Hayes (1995).
4. Bureau of the Census (1994).
5. Ceci (1991).
6. Mosteller (1995).

Chapter 7

1. Support for the preparation of this chapter was provided by a grant from the National Institute on Aging, IT50 AG11711-01.

Chapter 8

1. Quoted in Bob Herbert, "Call to Arms," *New York Times*, May 15, 1995, p. E15.

References

Preface

Bronfenbrenner, U. (1969, November 6). Statement at hearings before the Committee on Ways and Means, House of Representatives, 91st Congress, November 6, 1969. U.S. Government Printing Office, Washington: 1970, pp. 1837–1849.

Bronfenbrenner, U. (1975). Reality and research in the ecology of human development. *Proceedings of the American Philosophical Society, 119,* 439–469.

Chapter 1

Anderson, R.E., & Obershain, S.S. (1994). Cheating by students: Findings, reflections, and remedies. *Academic Medicine, 5,* 323–332.

Bastian, L. (1995). *Criminal victimization 1993.* Washington, DC: U.S. Department of Justice, Bureau of Justice Statistics.

Bastian, L., & Taylor, B.M. (1994). *Young black male victims.* Washington, DC: U.S. Department of Justice, Bureau of Justice Statistics.

Centers for Disease Control. (1991). Weapon-carrying among high school students—United States, 1990. *Morbidity and Mortality Weekly Report, 40,* 681–684.

Centers for Disease Control. (1994a). Health-risk behaviors among persons aged 12–21 years—United States, 1992. *Morbidity and Mortality Weekly Report, 43,* 231–235.

Centers for Disease Control. (1994b). Health-risk behaviors among adolescents who do and do not attend school—United States, 1992. *Morbidity and Mortality Weekly Report, 43,* 129–132.

Elliott, D.S., Huizinga, D., & Morse, B. (1987). Self-reported violent offending: A descriptive analysis of juvenile violent offenders and their offending careers. *Journal of Interpersonal Violence, 5,* 472–514.

Huizinga, D., Loeber, R., & Thornberry, T. (1993). Longitudinal study of delinquency, drug use, sexual activity, and pregnancy among children and youth in three cities. *Public Health Reports, 108,* 90–96.

Louis Harris and Associates. (1994). *The American teacher, 1993: Violence in America's public schools.* New York: Louis Harris and Associates.

Louis Harris and Associates. (1995). *The American teacher, 1994. Violence in America's public schools: The family perspective.* New York: Louis Harris and Associates.

McCabe, D.L., & Bowers, W.J. (1994). Academic dishonesty among males in college: A thirty year perspective. *Journal of College Student Development, 35,* 5–35.

Schab, F. (1991). Schooling without learning: Thirty years of cheating in high school. *Adolescence, 26,* 839–847.

Snyder, H.N., & Sickmund, M. (1995). *Juvenile offenders and victims: A national report.* Washington, DC: Office of Juvenile Justice and Delinquency Prevention.

Survey of California Lawyers. (1994, November). *California Bar Journal,* pp. 1, 6.

Survey Research Center. (1975–1992). *Monitoring the future.* Ann Arbor, MI: University of Michigan, Interuniversity Consortium for Political and Social Research.

U.S. Congress. Office of Technology Assessment. (1995). *Risks to students in school.* OTA-ENV-633. Washington, DC: U.S. Government Printing Office.

U.S. Department of Commerce, Bureau of the Census. (1994). *Current population reports, series P-20: Voting and registration in the election of 1992.* Washington, DC: U.S. Government Printing Office.

U.S. Department of Justice. (1991). *Teenage victims: A National Crime Survey report.* Washington, DC: Bureau of Justice Statistics.

Chapter 2

Beck, A.J., & Gilliard, D.C. (1993). *Jail inmates 1992.* Washington, DC: U.S. Department of Justice, Bureau of Justice Statistics.

Beck, A.J., & Gilliard, D.C. (1995). *Prisoners in 1994.* Washington, DC: U.S. Department of Justice, Bureau of Justice Statistics.

Beck, A.J., & Greenfeld, L. (1995). *Violent offenders in state prisons: Sentences and time served.* Washington, DC: U.S. Department of Justice, Bureau of Justice Statistics.

Beck, A.J., & Shipley, B.E.. (1989). *Recidivism of prisoners released in 1983.* Washington, DC: U.S. Department of Justice, Bureau of Justice Statistics.

Biderman, A.D., & Lynch, J.P. (1991). *Understanding crime incidence statistics: Why the UCR diverges from the NCS.* New York: Springer-Verlag.

Blumstein, A. (1995). Violence by young people: Why the deadly nexus? *National Institute of Justice Journal* (on-line edition), no. 299.

Cahalan, M.W. (1986). *Historical corrections statistics in the United States, 1850–1984.* Washington, DC: U.S. Department of Justice, Bureau of Justice Statistics.

Canadian Centre for Social Statistics. (1992). *Adult correctional services in Canada.* Ottawa: Minister of Supply and Services.

Center on Juvenile and Criminal Justice. (1995). *Trading books for bars: The lopsided funding battle between prisons and universities.* San Francisco: Center on Juvenile and Criminal Justice.

Council of Economic Advisors. (1994–1995). *Annual report to the president.* Washington, DC: U.S. Government Printing Office.

Council of Europe. (1992). *Prison information bulletin.* Strasbourg: Council of Europe.

Dembo, R., Hughes, P., Jackson, L., & Mieczkowski, T. (1993). Crack cocaine dealing by adolescents in two public housing projects: A pilot study. *Human Organization, 52,* 89–96.

Fagan, J. (1992). Drug selling and illicit income in distressed neighborhoods: The economic lives of street-level drug users and dealers. In A.V. Harrell & G.E. Peterson (eds.), *Drugs, crime and social isolation* (pp. 99–146). Washington, DC: Urban Institute Press.

Freeman, R.B. (1991). *Crime and the employment of disadvantaged youths.* Cambridge, MA: National Bureau of Economic Research.

Gilliard, D.K., & Beck, A.J. (1994). *Prisoners in 1993.* Washington, DC: U.S. Department of Justice, Bureau of Justice Statistics.

Klaus, P. (1994). *The costs of crime to victims: Crime data brief.* Washington, DC: U.S. Department of Justice, Bureau of Justice Statistics.

Langan, P.A. (1988). *Historical statistics on prisoners in state and federal institutions, yearend 1925–86.* Washington, DC: U.S. Department of Justice, Bureau of Justice Statistics.

MacKellar, F.L., & Yanagishita, M. (1995). *Homicide in the United States: Who's at risk?* Washington, DC: Population Research Bureau.

National Center for Health Statistics, Centers for Disease Control. (1993–1995). *Health United States.* Washington, DC: U.S. Government Printing Office.

New York Times. (1995, August 19). More in the U.S. are in prisons, report says.

Perkins, C.A., Stephan, J.J., & Beck, A.J. (1994). *Jails and jail inmates 1993–1994.* Washington, DC: U.S. Department of Justice, Bureau of Justice Statistics.

Piehl, A.M. (1994). *Learning while doing time.* Boston: Malcolm Weiner Center for Social Policy.

Shikita, M., & Tsuchiya, S. (eds.). (1992). *Crime and criminal policy in Japan.* New York: Springer-Verlag.

Snell, T. (1993). *Correctional populations in the United States, 1992.* Washington, DC: U.S. Department of Justice, Bureau of Justice Statistics.

Snyder, H.N., & Sickmund, M. (1995). *Juvenile offenders and victims: A national report.* Washington, DC: Office of Juvenile Justice and Delinquency Prevention.

United Nations. (1993). *Demographic yearbook 1992.* New York: United Nations.

U.S. Bureau of the Census. (1995). *Current population reports. Series P-25, Population estimates and projections.* Washington, DC: U.S. Government Printing Office.

U.S. Department of Commerce. (1965–1992). *State government finances.* Washington, DC: U.S. Government Printing Office.

U.S. Department of Justice. (1960–1994). *Crime in the United States* (Uniform Crime Reports). Washington, DC: Federal Bureau of Investigation.

U.S. Department of Justice. (1992). *Justice expenditure and employment, 1990.* Washington, DC: Bureau of Justice Statistics.

U.S. Department of Justice. (1995a). *Jail inmates 1994.* Washington, DC: Bureau of Justice Statistics.

U.S. Department of Justice. (1995b). *Sourcebook of criminal justice statistics, 1994.* Washington, DC: Bureau of Justice Statistics.

Walinsky, A. (1995, July). The crisis of public order. *Atlantic Monthly*, pp. 39–54.

World Health Organization. (1981–1993). *World health statistics annual.* New York: United Nations.

Chapter 3

American business survey. (1995, September 16). *Economist*, p. 18.

Bosworth, B. (1995, April 26). Private communication.

Burtless, G. (1995, June). International trade and the rise in earnings inequality. *Journal of Economic Literature, 33,* 800–816.

Karier, T. (1995, August). Technology: The R&D gap. *Challenge*, pp. 60–63.

Stein, H., and Foss, M. (1995). *The new illustrated guide to the American economy.* Washington, DC: AEI Press.

Wolff, E.N. (1995, Summer). International comparisons of personal wealth inequality. *American Prospect*, no. 22, pp. 58–64.

Zinsmeister, K. (1995, September–October). Payday mayday. *American Enterprise.*

Chapter 4

Bureau of Labor Statistics. (1950–1976; 1996). Unpublished reports and data tables.

Bureau of Labor Statistics. (1977–1988). *Handbook of labor statistics.* Washington, DC: U.S. Department of Labor.

Casper, L. (1995). *Current population reports: Household economic studies: What does it cost to mind our preschoolers?* Series P-70. Washington, DC: U.S. Department of Commerce, Bureau of the Census.

Department for Economic and Social Information and Policy Analysis. (1994). *Demographic yearbook: 1992.* New York: United Nations.

Dryfoos, J.G. (1990). *Adolescents at risk.* New York: Oxford University Press.

Hayes, C. (1987). *Risking the future: Adolescent sexuality, pregnancy and childbearing.* Washington, DC: National Academy Press.

Hobbs, F. (1990). *Children's well-being: An international comparison.* Washington, DC: U.S. Department of Commerce, Bureau of the Census.

Luster, T. & Small, S.A. (1990, May). *Youth at risk for teenage parenthood.* Paper presented at the Creating Caring Communities Conference, East Lansing, MI.

National Center for Health Statistics. (1959–1995). *Vital statistics of the United States, 1959–1991,* Vol 1: *Natality.* Washington, DC: Public Health Service.

National Center for Health Statistics. (1964–1994). *Vital statistics of the United States, 1960–1990.* Vol. 3: *Marriage and Divorce.* Washington, DC: U.S. Government Printing Office.

National Center for Health Statistics. (1994–1995). *Advance report of final natality statistics, 1992–1993.* Monthly Vital Statistics Report. Hyattsville, MD: National Center for Health Statistics.

National Research Council. (1987). *Risking the future: Adolescent sexuality, pregnancy, and childbearing,* Washington, DC: National Academy Press.

U.S. Bureau of the Census. (1960–1995). *Marital status and living arrangements: 1959–1994.* Current Population Reports, Series P-20. Washington, DC: U.S. Government Printing Office.

U.S. Bureau of the Census (1996). Unpublished 1994 data tables.

Ventura, S. (1995). *Births to unmarried mothers: United States, 1980–92 Vital Health Statistics, 21.*

Warren, R., & Passel, J. (1987). A count of the uncountable: Estimates of undocumented aliens counted in the 1980 United States Census. *Demography, 24* (3).

Woodrow, K. (1992). A consideration of the effects of immigration reform on the number of undocumented residents in the United States. *Population Research and Policy Review, 11, 117–144.*

Chapter 5

Children's Defense Fund. (1992). *The state of America's children.* Washington, DC: Children's Defense Fund.

National Center for Children in Poverty (1993). *Young children in poverty: A statistical update.* New York: Columbia University School of Public Health.

Rainwater, L. (1992) "Why the U.S. Antipoverty system doesn't work very well" *Challenge,* Jan/Feb. pp. 30–35.

Rainwater, L., & Smeeding, T. (1995a). *U.S. doing poorly—Compared with others.* New York: National Center for Children in Poverty, Columbia University School of Public Health.

Rainwater, L., & Smeeding, T. (1995b). *Doing poorly: The real income of American children in a comparative perspective.* Luxembourg Income Study Working Paper Series. Working Paper Series. Working Paper No. 127. Walferdange, Luxembourg: Center for Population, Poverty and Public Policy.

U.S. Bureau of the Census. (1961–1993). *Current population reports: Consumer income, series P-60, 1959–1992.* Washington, DC: U.S. Government Printing Office.

U.S. Bureau of the Census. (1960–1992). *Statistical abstract of the United States.* Washington, DC: U.S. Government Printing Office.

U.S. Bureau of the Census. (1993). *Measuring the effect of benefits and taxes on income and poverty.* Washington DC: U.S. Government Printing Office.

U.S. Bureau of the Census. (1961–1993). *Current population reports: Consumer income: Poverty in the United States: 1993,* series P-60, 1959–1992. Washington, DC: U.S. Government Printing Office.

U.S. Bureau of the Census. (1996). Unpublished data tables.

Woodrow, K. (1992). A consideration of the effects of immigration reform on the number of undocumented residents in the United States. *Population Research and Policy Review, 11,* 117–144.

Chapter 6

Barton, P., & Lapointe, A. (1995). *Indicators of performance in higher education* Princeton, NJ: Educational Testing Service.

Ceci, S.J. (1991). How much can we boost intelligence and its cognitive components? *Developmental Psychology, 27,* 703–722.

Elley, W.B. (1994). *The IEA study of reading literacy.* New York: Pergamon.

General Accounting Office. (1990, September). *Training strategies: Preparing non-college youth for employment in the U.S. and foreign countries.* Washington, DC: U.S. Government Printing Office.

Grissmer, D.W., Kirby, S.N., Berends, M., & Williamson, S. (1994). *Student achievement and the changing American family.* Rand Institute on Education and Training. Santa Monica, CA: Rand.

Kirsch, I., et al. (1993). *Adult literacy in America.* Princeton, NJ: Educational Testing Service.

Koretz, D. (1992). What happened to test scores and why? *Educational Measurement: Issues and Practice,* pp. 7–11.

The Mathematics Report Card. (1994). Princeton, NJ: Educational Testing Service.

McMillen, M.M., Kaufman, P., & Whitener, S. (1994, September). *Dropout rates in the United States: 1993.* U.S. Department of Education, Office of Educational Research and Improvement. Washington, DC: U.S. Government Printing Office.

Mosteller, F. (1995, May 30). *The Tennessee study of class size in the early school grades.* Cambridge, MA: American Academy of Arts and Sciences.

Ravitch, D. (1995). *National standards in education: A citizen's guide.* Washington, DC: Brookings Institution.

Robitaille, D.F., & Garden, R.A. (1989). *The IEA study of mathematics II: Contexts and outcomes of school mathematics.* New York: Pergamon Press.

Stevenson, H.W., & Stigler, J.W. (1992). *The learning gap: Why our schools are failing and what we can learn from Japanese and Chinese education.* New York: Summitt Books.

U.S. Bureau of the Census. (1994, August). *More education means higher career earnings.* Statistical brief, SB/94-17. Washington, DC: U.S. Government Printing Office.

U.S. Department of Education. National Center for Educational Statistics. (1990). *NAEP, Mathematics almanac.* Washington, DC: U.S. Government Printing Office.

U.S. Department of Education. National Center for Education Statistics (1993). *Digest of education statistics.* Washington, DC: U.S. Government Printing Office.

Zill, N. (1992, August). *Trends in family life and school performance.* Paper presented at the annual meeting of the American Sociological Association. Pittsburgh.

Chapter 7

Carnevale, A.P., & Stone, S.C. (1994). Developing the new competitive workforce. In J.A. Auerbach & J.C. Welsh (eds.), *Aging and competition: Rebuilding the U.S. workforce* (pp. 94–146). Washington, DC: National Planning Association.

Clymer, A. (1995, October 26). Americans reject big Medicare cuts, a new poll finds. *New York Times/CBS News Poll*, p. A1, D23–24.

The Commonwealth Fund. (1993). *The untapped resource: The final report of the Americans over 55 at Work Program.* New York: The Commonwealth Fund, Inc.

The Commonwealth Fund. (1993). *Building the competitive workforce: Investing in human capital for corporate success, Americans over 55 at Work Program,* New York: The Commonwealth Fund, Inc.

Congressional Budget Office. (1995, January). *The economic and budget outlook: Fiscal years 1996–2000.* Washington, DC: U.S. Government Printing Office.

Darnay, Arsen, J. (ed.) (1994). *Statistical record of older Americans.* Detroit: Gale Research.

Erikson, E. H., Erikson, J. M., & Kivnick, H. Q. (1986). *Vital involvement in old age.* New York: Norton.

Federal Old-Age and Survivors Insurance and Disability Trust Funds. Board of Trustees. (1995). *Annual report.* Washington, DC: U.S. Government Printing Office.

Fields, G. S., & Mitchell, O. S. (1994). *Retirement, pensions, and social security.* Cambridge, MA: MIT Press.

Graebner, W. (1980). *A history of retirement.* New Haven: Yale University Press.

Hall, D.T., & Mirvis, P.H. (1994). The new workplace and older Workers. In J.A. Auerbach & J.C. Welsh (eds.), *Aging and competition: Rebuilding the U.S. workforce* (pp. 58–93). Washington, DC: National Planning Association.

Han, Shin-kap. (1996). Structuring relations in on-the-job networks. *Social Networks, 18,* 47–67.

Kahn, R.L. (1994). Opportunities, aspirations, and goodness of fit. In M.W. Riley, R.L. Kahn, & A. Foner (eds.), *Age and structural lag* (pp. 37–56). New York: Wiley-Interscience.

Kahne, H. (1985). *Reconceiving part-time work.* Totowa, NJ: Rowman and Allanheld.

Kaiser Commission on the Future of Medicaid. (1995, July). *Medicaid: The health and long-term care safety net.* Washington, DC: U.S. Government Printing Office.

Korczyk, S.M. (1993). Gender issues in employer pensions policy. In R.V. Burkhauser & D.L. Salisbury (eds.), *Pensions in a changing economy* (pp. 59–66). Washington, DC: National Institute on Aging.

Marshall, R. (1994). A new social contract. In J.A. Auerbach & J.C. Welsh (eds.), *Aging and competition: Rebuilding the U.S. workforce* (pp. 207–224). Washington, DC: National Planning Association.

McNaught, W. (1994). Realizing the potential: Some examples. In M.W. Riley, R.L. Kahn, & A. Foner (eds.), *Age and structural lag* (pp. 219–236). New York: John Wiley & Sons.

Merton, R. K. (1968). *Social theory and social structure.* New York: Free Press.

Moen, P. (1994). Women, work, and family: A sociological perspective on changing roles. In M.W. Riley, R.L. Kahn, & A. Foner (eds.), *Age and structural lag* (pp. 151–170). New York: John Wiley & Sons.

Moen, P. (1995). A life course approach to post-retirement roles and well-being. In L. A. Bond, S. J. Cutler, & A. Grams (eds.), *Promoting successful and productive aging* (pp. 230–257). Thousand Oaks, CA: Sage.

Moen, P., Dempster-McClain, D., & Williams, R. M. (1992). Successful aging: A life course perspective on women's health. *American Journal of Sociology, 97,* 1612–1638.

National Center for Health Statistics. (1990). *Current estimates from the National Health Interview Survey, 1989.* Vital and Health Statistics, Series 10, No. 176. Hyattsville, MD: Public Health Service.

National Center for Health Statistics. (1991). *Health United States, 1990.* Hyattsville, MD: Public Health Service.

National Center for Health Statistics. (1991–1992). *Vital statistics.* Hyattsville, MD: Public Health Service.

National Center for Health Statistics, Centers for Disease Control. (1993). *National hospital discharge study.* Hyattsville, MD: Public Health Service.

National Center for Health Statistics. (1994). *Health United States, 1993.* Hyattsville, MD: Public Health Service.

National Center for Health Statistics. (1995a) *Healthy People 2000 Review, 1994.* Hyattsville, MD: Public Health Service.

National Center for Health Statistics. (1995b) *Health United States, 1994.* Hyattsville, MD: Public Health Service.

New York Times. (1995, March 26).

Pechman, J.A., Aaron, H.J., & Tausig, M.K. (1968). *Social security: Perspectives for reform.* Washington, DC: Brookings Institution.

Quinn, J.F., & Burkhauser, R.V. (1990). Work and retirement. In R.H. Binstock & L.K. George (Eds.), *Handbook of aging and the social sciences* (3rd edition, pp. 307–327). San Diego, CA: Academic Press.

Radner, Daniel B. (1991). Changes in the incomes of age groups, 1984–1989, *Social Security Bulletin, 54* (12), Table 8.

Reno, V.P. (1993). The role of pension in retirement income. In R.V. Burkhauser & D.L. Salisbury (eds.), *Pensions in a changing economy* (pp. 19–32). Washington, DC: National Institute on Aging.

Riley, M.W., Kahn, R.L., & Foner, A. (1994). *Age and structural lag.* New York: John Wiley & Sons.

Riley, M.W., & Riley, J.W., Jr. (1994). Structural lag: Past and future. In M.W. Riley, R. Kahn, & A. Foner (eds.), *Age and structural lag* (pp. 15–36). New York: John Wiley & Sons.

Salisbury, Dallas, L. (1993). Policy implications of changes in employer pension protection. In R.V. Burkhauser & D.L. Salisbury (eds.), *Pensions in a changing economy* (pp. 41–58). Washington, DC: National Institute on Aging.

Schulz, J.H. (1988). *The economics of aging.* Dover, MA: Auburn House.

Social Security Administration, (1994), *Annual statistical supplement to the Social Security Bulletin,* Washington, DC: U.S. Government Printing Office.

Synder, Donald, C. (1993). The economic well-being of retired workers by race and Hispanic origin. In R.V. Burkhauser & D.L. Salisbury (eds.), *Pensions in a changing economy* (pp. 67–78). Syracuse, NY: National Academy on Aging, Syracuse University.

Tragash, H.J. (1994). A corporate perspective on competitiveness and aging workers. In J.A. Auerbach & J.C. Welsh (eds.), *Aging and competition: Rebuilding the U.S. workforce* (pp. 147–165). Washington, DC: National Planning Association.

U.S. Bureau of the Census. (1975). *Historical statistics of the United States, colonial times to 1970.* Bicentennial ed., pt. 1, Washington, DC: U.S. Government Printing Office, (1995).

U.S. Bureau of the Census. (1995). The 1989 American housing survey. Data on CD-ROM.

U.S. Bureau of the Census. (1991). *Poverty in the United States: 1990.* Current Population Reports, Series P-60, No. 175. Washington, DC: U.S. Government Printing Office.

U.S. Bureau of the Census. (1992). *Sixty-five in the United States.* Current Population Reports, Washington, DC: U.S. Government Printing Office.

U.S. Bureau of the Census. (1994a). *Marital status and living arrangements.* Current Population Reports, Series P20–478, Washington, DC: U.S. Government Printing Office.

U.S. Bureau of the Census. (1994b) *Statistical abstracts of the United States.* Washington, DC: U.S. Government Printing Office.

U.S. Bureau of the Census. (1994c). *Current population reports.* Series P-20, 45, 77, 99, 121, 138, 158, 169, 182, 274, 356, 415, 451, 476; Series P-25, No. 98, 310, 519, 917, 1018, 1045. Washington, DC: U.S. Government Printing Office.

U.S. Bureau of the Census. (1995, May). *Sixty-five in the United States.* Current Population Reports. Washington, DC: Government Printing Office.

U.S. Bureau of Data Management and Strategy, Health Care Financing Administration. (1996). Unpublished data.

U.S. Bureau of Labor Statistics. (1988). *Labor force statistics derived from the current population survey, 1948–87.* Bulletin 2307. Washington, DC: U.S. Government Printing Office.

U.S. Bureau of Labor Statistics. (1990). *Displaced workers, 1987–1991: Recession swells count of displaced workers.* Bulletin 2427. Washington, DC: U.S. Government Printing Office.

U.S. Bureau of Labor Statistics. (1993). Thirty-eight million persons do volunteer work. Press release. USDL, 90–145. Data are from May 1989 Current Population Survey.

U.S. Congress. House Select Committee on Aging. (1992). *Elderly households, A profile.* Report 102-912, 102d Congress, 2nd session.

U.S. Department of Health and Human Services. Social Security Administration.

(1993). *Annual statistical supplement, 1992, to the Social Security Bulletin.* Washington, DC: U.S. Government Printing Office.

U.S. Department of Health and Human Services. Social Security Administration. (1994). *Annual statistical supplement, 1994, to the Social Security Bulletin.* Washington, DC: U.S. Government Printing Office.

U.S. Department of Labor, Bureau of Labor Statistics. (1992). *Outlook 1990–2005,* BLS Bulletin 2402, May. Washington, DC: U.S. Government Printing Office.

U.S. Department of Labor. (1994). *Report on the American workforce.* Washington, DC: U.S. Government Printing Office.

U.S. General Accounting Office. (1990). *Age discrimination: Use of age-specific provisions in company exit incentive programs.* Washington, DC: U.S. Government Printing Office.

U.S. Senate Special Committee on Aging, the American Association of Retired Persons, the Federal Council on Aging, and the U.S. Administration on Aging. (1991). *Aging America: Trends and projections.* Washington, DC: U.S. Department of Health and Human Services.

Useem, M. (1994). Business restructuring and the aging workforce. In J.A. Auerbach & J.C. Welsh (eds.), *Aging and competition: Rebuilding the U.S. workforce* (pp. 33–57). Washington, DC: National Planning Association.

Acknowledgments

W e owe a special indebtedness to Susan Arellano, our editor, for her vision, wisdom, patience, and support in this endeavor. Without her, it would have never become a reality. We also acknowledge the advice and generosity of demographers and senior staff in the following government agencies: Arlene Saluter, Bureau of Marriage and Family Statistics; Ellie Baugher, Poverty and Health Branch; Stephanie Ventura and Catherine Short, Bureau of Vital Statistics; Randy Ilg, Bureau of Labor Statistics; and Sally C. Clarke, Division of Vital Statistics. Special gratitude is expressed to the following senior demographers who provided guidance, wise counsel, and invaluable unpublished data over the course of three decades: Howard Haygye, Robert Heuser, Don Hernandez, and Arthur Norton. J. Lawrence Aber and Jaili Li, of the National Center for Children in Poverty, also provided critical assistance. We express our appreciation to the following colleagues in the College of Human Ecology of Cornell University for their advice and practical assistance, particularly in the early stages of the project: Dean Francille Firebaugh, Richard L. Canfield, John Eckenrode, James Garbarino, Jennifer Gerner, and Stephen F. Hamilton. A distinctive feature of the enterprise was the active participation of the following undergraduate students in all phases of this endeavor: Briana Barocas, Terri M. Burger, Nell Eppinger, Suzanne Epstein, Alexis Krulish, Vivian Nirenblatt, Jessica Schwarting, Elizabeth

Scotto, Heidi Shydo, Sean Siegel, Bonnie Sihler, and Carrie Wasserman. We owe an unreimbursable debt to staff of the Cornell University Library, in particular, Stuart Basefsky, Tom Clausen, and Gregory Lawrence. Maggie Mateer and Delmy Perez and especially Albert Ting contributed in critical ways to the organization and analysis of the enormous bodies of data on which we drew and preparation of graphs. Mark Ehlen and Kim Rosenstein organized the data for chapters 3 and 7, respectively. Finally, there are two persons who contributed to the organization and coordination of the whole endeavor. The first, Elliott Smith, served as the administrative coordinator in the difficult early phases of the project; the second, Gerri Jones, has served, in effect, as the administrator of the project through its entirety. Without their vision, encouragement, good humor, and unwavering support in times of crisis, this book would have never seen the light of day. This undertaking was supported by the Bronfenbrenner Life Course Center under the direction of Phyllis Moen. Special thanks are extended to Dean Francille Firebaugh of Cornell University's College of Human Ecology for financial support, unfailing encouragement, and wise counsel.

Finally, acknowledgment is extended to Liese Bronfenbrenner and Richard Shore, for contributions that only they could have made.